COVENANT • BIBLE • STUDIES

The Gospel of Mark

Frank Ramirez

faithQuest® ◆ Brethren Press®

Cover photo by Vista III Design, Inc.

00 99 98 97 96   5 4 3 2 1

Library of Congress Cataloging-in-Publication Data

Ramirez, Frank, 1954-
      The Gospel of Mark / Frank Ramirez.
            p.   cm.
      Includes bibliographical references.
      ISBN 0-87178-321-5 (alk. paper)
      1. Bible. N.T. Mark—Criticism, interpretation, etc. 2. Bible. N.T. Mark—Study and teaching. I. Title.
BS2585.2.R34   1996   95-42590
226.3'06—dc20

Manufactured in the United States of America

Contents

Foreword

The Covenant Bible Study Series was first developed for a denominational program in the Church of the Brethren and the Christian Church (Disciples of Christ). This program, called People of the Covenant, was founded on the concept of relational Bible study and has been adopted by several other denominations and small groups who want to study the Bible in a community rather than alone.

Relational Bible study is marked by certain characteristics, some of which differ from other types of Bible study. For one, it is intended for small groups of people who can meet face-to-face on a regular basis and share frankly with an intimate group.

It is important to remember that relational Bible study is anchored in covenantal history. God covenanted with people in Old Testament history, established a new covenant in Jesus Christ, and covenants with the church today.

Relational Bible study takes seriously a corporate faith. As each person contributes to study, prayer, and work, the group becomes the real body of Christ. Each one's contribution is needed and important. "For just as the body is one and has many members, and all the members of the body, though many, are one body, so it is with Christ. ... Now you are the body of Christ and individually members of it" (1 Cor. 12:12, 17).

Relational Bible study helps both individuals and the group to claim the promise of the Spirit and the working of the Spirit. As one person testified, "In our commitment to one another and in our sharing, something happened. ... We were woven together in love by the master Weaver. It is something that can happen only when two or three or seven are gathered in God's name, and we know the promise of God's presence in our lives."

The symbol for these covenant Bible study groups is the burlap cross. The interwoven threads, the uniqueness of each strand, the unrefined fabric, and the rough texture characterize covenant groups. The people in the groups are unique but interrelated; they are imperfect and unpolished, but loving and supportive.

The shape that these divergent threads create is the cross, the symbol for all Christians of the resurrection and presence with us of Christ our Savior. Like the burlap cross, we are brought together, simple and ordinary, to be sent out again in all directions to be in the world.

For people who choose to use this study in a small group, the following guidelines will help create an atmosphere in which support will grow and faith will deepen.

1. As a small group of learners, we gather around God's word to discern its meaning for today.
2. The words, stories, and admonitions we find in scripture come alive for today, challenging and renewing us.
3. All people are learners and all are leaders.
4. Each person will contribute to the study, sharing the meaning found in the scripture and helping to bring meaning to others.
5. We recognize each other's vulnerability as we share out of our own experience, and in sharing we learn to trust others and to be trustworthy.

Additional suggestions for study and group-building are provided in the "Sharing and Prayer" section. They are intended for use in the hour preceding the Bible study to foster intimacy in the covenant group and relate personal sharing to the Bible study topic.

Welcome to this study. As you search the scriptures, may you also search yourself. May God's voice and guidance and the love and encouragement of brothers and sisters in Christ challenge you to live more fully the abundant life God promises.

Preface

The Gospel of Mark was probably written around 60 A.D. by a fellow who appears here and there throughout the scriptures. He is mentioned by name in several books of the New Testament, but in his own account of Jesus' life and teachings, his appearances are only speculative. For the most part, he does not intrude in his own story.

Of the two places he may appear in the gospel, the first is Mark 14:13. In preparation for the last supper, Jesus "sent two of his disciples, saying to them, 'Go into the city, and a man carrying a jar of water will meet you; follow him ....'" Apparently the meeting place of the early church and the location of the last supper was in the home of Mark's mother (Acts 12:12). The man carrying the jar could have been Mark himself, meeting the disciples. Since women generally carried water, any man carrying such a jar would have stood out and was obviously meant as a signal to the disciples. Maybe his mother sent him out to meet the others.

The second supposed appearance of Mark in his own story comes in Mark 14:51-52. Here we read: "A young man, wearing nothing but a linen garment, was following Jesus. When they seized him, he fled naked, leaving his garment behind" (NIV). The fact the young man was wearing no undergarments means he had dressed hastily. Some feel this is Mark's signature, letting us know he was quick to be at his Savior's side at that terrible time.

The other appearances are in other writers' accounts. In Acts 12:25; 13:13; and 15:37-39, Mark appears as a companion of Paul and Barnabas, but he left the missionary journey early, perhaps because of homesickness, exhaustion, or other commitments. We get the impression that Paul was impatient with Mark's departure and that there were lasting feelings of anger and alienation. Yet in Philemon 24; Colossians 4:10; and 2 Timothy 4:11, Paul mentions Mark as his companion in prison. Things were patched up. Then in 1 Peter 5:13, Mark is referred to as "my son." This is probably meant in the sense that Mark came to accept Jesus as Lord and Savior through Peter.

Like Mark, we have all been alienated and reconciled at times. Also, like him, we are sometimes on the edge of great events. Although we are not movers and shakers, we should in similar fashion seek to point others not to ourselves, but to the risen Lord, Jesus Christ. Jesus is our source and our being. Jesus is the true author of all good things. If we can be mirrors of these great events, focusing the attention on Jesus, then we will have been as faithful as Mark in our witness.

—Frank Ramirez

Recommended Resources

Barclay, William. *The Gospel of Mark* (Daily Study Bible Series). Westminster John Knox, 1956.

Nouwen, Henri. *Walk with Jesus: Stations of the Cross*. Orbis Books, 1990.

Williamson, Lamar, Jr. *Mark* (Interpretation Series). Westminster John Knox, 1983.

1

The Beginning of the Good News
Mark 1—16

Mark wants us to know Jesus, but we cannot know Jesus unless we know all parts of his life and ministry from beginning to end. So Mark gives us a summary at the beginning of his book and then spins out the whole story in more detail. We only know dimly until we get to the cross and resurrection.

Personal Preparation

1. Read the entire Gospel of Mark. Use a modern English translation (New Revised Standard Version, Contemporary English Version, or *The Message*). Try to read it in one gulp. If your Bible is not a family heirloom, mark up the text as you read. Look for themes, incidents, and story techniques that are repeated.
2. When you finish your reading, write down the major themes you found and stories from the other gospels that are missing in Mark. Note the names for Jesus that Mark uses at the beginning of the book and at the end of the book. Also write down what is for you the most unusual thing about Mark's story.
3. Reflect on the questions, What does Jesus Christ have to do with my life today? this week?

Understanding

To my mind there are two ways to tell a story.

My sister-in-law (whom I love dearly) will not let you know how a story ends until you travel with her the whole way through the tale. She will start at the beginning (as Lewis Carroll once advised), keep on going until she reaches the end, then stop.

The trouble with my sister-in-law's style is that through the whole telling you do not know how things come out, and it leads to a lot of anxiety that might be unnecessary if the story has a happy ending.

When I have something to tell someone, I begin by saying "Everything's okay, but ... ," and then I proceed to say how so-and-so had to go to the hospital, or an unexpected bill came that day, or there was a phone call from somebody saying they were in trouble. By saying everything is okay, I let my listener know that everything is all worked out, so don't be frightened.

Mark used both techniques in his gospel. Right from the beginning he told us there is Good News about Jesus, that it was predicted in the Scriptures, and that everything is okay. On the other hand, you will have to travel with him through the whole story before you understand everything. You cannot jump to any conclusions. That is why it will be helpful to take time to read the gospel the whole way through.

Most authorities agree that Mark is the first "gospel" as we know it. It is quite likely that there were other collections of the sayings of Jesus circulating either in written or oral form, although none of those predating the four gospels has survived.

Mark collected sayings and stories about Jesus and arranged them in what he called the "good news" (from which we derive the word *gospel*) about Jesus Christ. In doing so he created a new form of literature that was more than biography. He wanted to do more than tell a life story. Mark wanted to define Jesus' life in terms of God's story.

There are many theories about the origin of the Gospel of Mark. An early Christian named Papias wrote a book between 120-130 A.D., which has been lost but was widely quoted by others. In it, he claimed that Mark used the stories that Peter told about Jesus to put together his gospel. Other theories place Mark in Rome when he wrote his book.

Dating any book of the Bible can be difficult. Occasionally, however, verses mention specific historical events that help us know when the Scripture was written. For instance, an important event for dating New Testament writings is the destruction of the Temple in Jerusalem, which took place during the Jewish War (67 and 71 A.D.). Some scholars believe there are no clues in Mark that even remotely refer to the fall of Jerusalem. So it would seem the book was written before the fall. There does seem to be an awareness in Mark, however, that trouble was on the way. As a result some date the Gospel of Mark around 65-67 A.D.

The author of Mark was silent. He did not give us a first person account or suggest that these were his personal experiences. But on two occasions, Mark may make an appearance in the gospel. The first possible appearance is in 14:13, "So [Jesus] sent two of his disciples, saying to them, 'Go into the city, and a man carrying a jar of water will meet you; follow him .' "

The home of Mark's mother was identified in Acts 12:12 as the meeting place of the early church and possibly as the location of the last supper. For this reason some suppose it might have been Mark himself who met the disciples. Since women generally carried water, any man bearing a jar (probably in a clumsy fashion) would have stood out, a clear signal to the disciples. Perhaps his mother sent Mark out to meet them.

Shortly after the arrest of Jesus, we read of a possible second appearance: "A certain young man was following him, wearing nothing but a linen cloth. They caught hold of him, but he left the linen cloth and ran off naked." (14:51-52) The fact that the young man was wearing no undergarments meant he had dressed hastily, perhaps reacting to the news of Jesus' arrest. Some feel this is Mark's signature, letting us know he was there at that terrible time.

There are other New Testament references to Mark. In Acts 12:25; 13:13; and 15:37-39, he appeared as a traveling companion with Paul and Barnabas. But Mark left the missionary journey early, perhaps because of homesickness, exhaustion, or other commitments. Later when Barnabas suggested they take Mark on another evangelistic journey, Paul refused to take "a deserter." They disagreed sharply and parted company, Paul choosing Silas as a companion and Barnabas taking Mark. The bad feelings did not last forever. In Philemon 24; Colossians

4:10; and 2 Timothy 4:11, Paul mentioned Mark as a companion. Things were patched up. Moreover, 1 Peter 5:13 referred to Mark as "my son." Questions of authorship aside, this is probably meant to commemorate the historic link between Mark and Peter.

Like Mark's, our own lives have their moments of alienation and reconciliation. Also like him, we are more often on the edge of great events than at the center of them. We are not movers and shakers, but we can, like Mark, point others to the risen Lord, Jesus Christ, who is at the center. He is the source of our being, the author of all good things. If we can be mirrors of these great events, focusing the attention on Jesus, and not on ourselves, then we will have been as faithful as Mark in our witness.

You have read *what* was written in the Gospel of Mark. Perhaps you wonder *why* it was written. At the first church I served as pastor, the Ladera Church of the Brethren in Los Angeles, we were very fortunate to have a member Doris Forney who had a real sense of history. She took time to prepare elaborate scrapbooks containing all the early records of the congregation, along with photographs she meticulously labeled. Although at the time the book was filled with stuff "everybody knew," it proved invaluable for people who came along later, especially as older members moved away or died.

Mark seems to have lived in a time when the original witnesses to the life of Jesus began to die. No doubt there was a time when everyone knew this stuff, and newcomers to the faith could hear this story directly from those who had been there. One of the reasons Mark wrote was probably to preserve the memories of those who had gone on before.

But that was not the only reason. Mark's true mission was to create followers for Jesus. Some Christians may be under the impression that the best way to get to know Jesus is to read about his life. We know from experience, however, that it is more important to establish a relationship with Christ and with God's people. It is more important to believe and follow than to know. Knowledge about his life can come later.

For Mark, the first thing to do was to confess that Jesus Christ is Lord. Then came the resolution to follow in his footsteps. The gospels were written to guide people who could confess that they believed in Jesus, not to convince nonbelievers. And they were written not to create believers, but to create disciples out of believers, those who walked in the pattern or image of Jesus. To Mark reality was simple. Jesus was Lord of the natural and spiritual realms. This included believers and nonbelievers on earth and God's servants in the spiritual realm, angels as well as demons directly opposed to God's will. Mark wanted his readers to understand that Jesus as the Christ, the Son of God, has a royal claim on our loyalties. This news is so important it must be told in the form of a gospel, or good news.

Mark wanted us to know who Jesus is, but he knew this was not possible unless we heard the whole story. That is why it was necessary for you to read the whole gospel before we began. In this way Mark was like my sister-in-law Nancy. But because this good news is so urgent, Mark told us everything at the start.

Mark began this way: "The beginning of the good news of Jesus Christ, the Son of God." These words alone contain all the major themes of the book. "The beginning" of the gospel means not only the start, but the foundation. The word for beginning contains the same root as the word for ruler and king, who was the individual upon whom society's well-being rested.

The word *gospel* means "Good News." The name Jesus makes it clear this is a person who really existed. His title, Christ (Messiah, the Anointed One), tells us that he is the one whom God's people have been expecting. The phrase Son of God is doubly significant. This title ties his divine nature to the humanity of his name. Claiming the title Son of God is the crime for which Jesus was executed. The Judean authorities found him guilty of blasphemy when he replied to the question, "Are you the Messiah, the Son of the Blessed One?" with the answer, "I am." (14:61-62) Only when we know the human Jesus of the crucifixion and the divine Christ of the resurrection do we fully know God's Son, at least according to Mark. Mark called him "Jesus Messiah, the Son of God." This is the Good News.

The first thing you may have noticed in your reading is that, compared to Luke and Matthew, Mark's gospel is fairly brief. Though an excellent storyteller, he excluded the story of Jesus' birth and most of the parables with which we are familiar. Mark plunged headlong into the tale, never allowing the reader a moment's rest through the tumultuous events of Passion Week, through the crucifixion, and beyond to the shattering events at the tomb.

The second thing that stands out is the great emphasis upon secrecy in the first half of the book. Why did Jesus want to keep his identity a secret? After all, aren't we supposed to be spreading the good news ("Go therefore and make disciples of all nations," Matt. 28:19)? But this is consistent with Mark's way of telling the story. We come to know Jesus Christ fully only through his death and resurrection. He cannot be known by his parts. That is, it is not enough to recognize Jesus as teacher, as miracle worker, and as healer. He is all of these, but he is the crucified God and risen Lord as well. This is the reason for what we know as the "Messianic Secret." When Jesus healed or performed a mighty work, he instructed those present to keep the secret. Partial knowledge about Jesus is just as false as no knowledge.

Halfway through the gospel things change. Despite the fact the disciples did not understand what had occurred in the miraculous feeding of the four thousand, Jesus asked the crucial question, "Who do people say that I am?" (8:27) This elicited Peter's confession: "You are the Messiah!" This is the only right answer, and with this knowledge it is possible to understand who Jesus is.

The word *messiah* literally means "the anointed one." Just as kings were anointed, so too the one coming in the name of God would be set apart in a special way. Jesus was the one who was long expected—and yet unexpected, for it was not immediately evident to his own people that he was the Messiah.

Ironically, in the Gospel of Mark the outsiders, the ones who were not close to Jesus, immediately recognized his lordship—from the demons he battled to the centurion who assisted in the execution. The insiders, the disciples and people closest to Jesus, were out of it. They did not get it.

What was really lacking in the Disciples' understanding was the cross. They did not want to think of the Messiah as a mere human who would suffer. When Jesus tried to tell them about it, they did not want to hear it. Without the cross, however, the kingdom makes no sense. The cross is the intersection between the kingdom and reality. It is the central point at which they converge.

The trick is for the reader to identify with both camps. When we are down and out, we are the lost people Jesus came to save. When we are smug and secure, we are the ones he came to warn. We can be touched and healed by him simply by recognizing his lordship. And we can reject his claims by refusing to make him Lord of our lives.

You may wonder, What has this to do with me? The Gospel of Mark directly challenges us to be disciples. This means we are to live like Jesus. Obviously, Jesus is a divine power. This is evident in the miracles of healing, feeding, and forgiving. But these are available to us only by rejecting earthly power and choosing a lifestyle in which suffering is possible. The road to the kingdom leads out of the gates of Jerusalem and to the hill of the skull.

And it is a road we are called to share as a community of believers.

Discussion and Action

1. What were your first impressions of Jesus? Did you come to know of him through nursery rhymes, Bible stories, pious paintings, or sermons?
2. Share with each other how it felt to read Mark's gospel through as one complete story. What themes did you find? What surprised you in this gospel?
3. Talk about some of the stories or parables that are missing in Mark's gospel.
4. In pairs, interview each other asking, "Who do people say Jesus is?" Then ask, "Who do *you* say that Jesus is?"
5. At what point in your life were you the most powerful, at least as the world judges? Do you still possess the same power? How do you understand the suffering servant model of Jesus' life? Name some ways you would be willing to give up control or power in your life to follow Jesus.
6. Discuss some of the changes in your thinking about Jesus over your lifetime. When did these changes occur? How do you still seek to understand Jesus and his way more fully? How is Jesus still a mystery to you?

2

The Time Is Up!
Mark 1:1-20

With the arrival of Jesus, a new era began. It is one in which the real King is going to be revealed and the kingdom is at least partially apparent. How shall we prepare?

Personal Preparation

1. Reread Mark 1:1-20. Pretend for a moment this is all of the gospel that exists. What could we learn of Jesus from these few verses alone?
2. Call to mind a beginning in your life—the moment you met a spouse, found a job, or became aware of your mortality. How did that moment make you who you are today? How did who you are affect that moment?
3. Where do you think God's kingdom can be found? Is it located in one place or time? Try writing down in a paragraph, a parable, or a number of statements what you believe about God's kingdom.

Understanding

In 1861, Wilmer McLean left his Virginia farm when a Union cannonball tore through his summer kitchen during the Battle of Bull Run, the first major conflict of the Civil War. In order to escape the madness, he moved to a small town known as Appomattox Court House. It was there, in his living room, that General Lee surrendered to General Grant three and one-half years later. He could truly say, "The war began in my front yard and ended in my front parlor."

In the same way, these few verses of Mark contain the beginning and the end of the gospel.

Seemingly out of the void came John the Immerser, who grabbed the attention of the people with sideshow techniques. Here was a man who appeared at the edge of the wilderness, the place of desolation and alienation, to call people to make their lives right. He came to a nation gilt with an ancient hope in a glorious promise, but which was occupied by a hated foreign power. *Africa - eat termites*

John wore strange clothes, ate bugs, and quoted from the songs that were sung by the people on their way back from exile in Babylon centuries before. He believed that the songs' promises of a Messiah were about to be fulfilled, so he called for repentance as a means of preparation.

In this context Jesus also appeared. He too is presented as a person from nowhere. Galilee had been Jewish only a relatively short time, and there was much ill will between that region and Judea. But when this ordinary peasant carpenter rose from the waters, he had an extraordinary experience called an epiphany (a word that means, "Look! There's God!"). His title as God's Son was confirmed by the highest authority.

Jesus was now the boss's son. I remember working at a plant where a number of managers' sons and daughters, including myself, put in time over the summer. What followed depended on the parent's philosophy. Some worked little, or not at all, yet drew a paycheck. I was told by my father, however, that being a manager's son meant working even harder than the others.

God seems to be that kind of parent. Before Jesus had the chance to bask in the glow of this personal recommendation, he was sent immediately into the wilderness.

What followed is a neat trick of reversal. Adam in Eden was tempted by Satan and sent out into the wilderness. Immediately after his baptism, Jesus also went to the wilderness, a place of alienation, desolation, the place where the people of the exodus spent a generation dying on their way to the promised land. There he was tempted by Satan. But he was able to resist the enticements, thus he restored Eden before the fall. The mention that Jesus "was with the wild beasts" implies not danger, but reconciliation. The harmony enjoyed by humanity and nature before the fall was restored.

Unlike the accounts in Matthew and Luke, Mark gave no details about the temptation of Jesus. What mattered was that the testing took place. Most of us resent times when we are pushed to the edge of our endurance. But these forty days of deprivation, corresponding to the forty years spent by God's children in the desert, were a benefit to Jesus. They made clear just what his ministry would be.

Trials, such as the time Jesus experienced in the wilderness, can make or break us. They certainly put the world in perspective. While none of us desires these things, we should not shrink from them either. As it was for Jesus, trials often help us know what our ministry to the world and our neighbors will be.

At least this was the conclusion of Paul Brand. His book *Pain: The Gift Nobody Wants* (co-authored with Philip Yancey) made the point that in his experience nothing of value is accomplished in life without some measure of pain or discomfort. He did not suggest that pain is desirable or pleasant. However, only by confronting and pushing the boundaries of comfort is it possible to become strong and have a lasting effect on the world.

Having spent his childhood in India, along with a significant portion of his adult life ministering to lepers, Brand compared the tolerance of pain in many developing countries to the indignation of wealthy countries when confronted by trials and tribulations. As citizens of one of the wealthiest countries in the world, our tendency is to seek immediate relief rather than use the pain as a diagnostic tool or point of growth.

No one is exempt from trials, including John the Immerser. His arrest effectively ended his ministry, but not before he baptized Jesus and gained Jesus' recognition.

The stage is set for the rest of the story in these verses taken from the translation known as the Scholars' Version: "After John was locked up, Jesus came to Galilee proclaiming God's good news. His message went: 'The time is up: God's imperial rule is closing in. Change your ways and put your trust in the good news!' " (1:14-15 Scholars' Version)

With the arrival of Jesus a new era began. It is one in which the real King is going to be revealed and the kingdom is at least partially apparent. This era is one of *kairos* time, a Greek word that transcends the chronological way of looking at things. It recognizes that the experience of duration has nothing to do with the ticking of the second hand. Time spent on your back during a root canal or riding out an earthquake tends to seem longer than birthdays and anniversaries. In *kairos* time we have entered a season that transcends every other way of marking the minutes.

The New Revised Standard Version says, "The kingdom of God has come near." This particular wording allows both meanings—the kingdom of God is near physically, and it is also on the way. It is fully present, yet not fully realized.

If the kingdom of God described in the gospel were tied to one place or time, the gospel would have been a failure. But time and place are only a part of the meaning of "kingdom." Originally the concept of kingdom was tied to one piece of ground, the promised land, which had its day during the rule of David and Solomon. Even though by our standards the territory wouldn't have made much of a dent in our eastern seaboard, the fact of its existence made it a golden age in the memory of the people who were first taken in exile to Babylon, then returned to the ruins of a land that seemed to have forgotten them. *"The kingdom of God is within you"*

The prophets Haggai and Zechariah, leaders in the rebuilding of the Temple after the Exile, spread God's revelation, reshaping the kingdom ideal. Under the Persians, God's people had freedom of religion and relative autonomy but they did not have a real king. The kingdom of God came to be redefined not as a special place, but a happening. God's realm included both heaven and earth, and although God's presence might not always be felt, God's authority would remain unquestioned, at least in the eyes of the people. Documents written under persecution, such as the Book of Daniel, looked ahead to a day when God's kingdom would become apparent to the whole world.

In Mark's gospel, the kingdom of God is not an either/or proposition. It is not a question of whether it exists now, or in the future. The answer is both. We are citizens of that kingdom and live in it now, but that will only become clear to everyone later. The authority of its King, Jesus, will become unquestioned in God's own time.

Coupled with the proclamation, "The time is up! The kingdom of God is at hand!" is a call to repentance. What does it mean to repent? How radical a change do we need to make? Jay Leno once said it was a good thing NASA was finally using women astronauts. At least now if the shuttle got lost, someone would stop and ask for directions. The concept of repentance implies we are going the wrong way. In order to get right we have to turn around. This does not mean that with repentance we are wholly well or that the process is done, but it does mean we are finally pointed the right way. The journey is by no means complete at this point. The questions raised by Jesus' followers make that clear. However, at least those who repent have stopped to ask for directions!

Mark concluded this part of his gospel with the call of the first disciples. Here is where we come into the story. There comes a certain moment when an opportunity is ripe. It may last only a short time. The phrase from Revelation works best: the time is near (*kairos engus*). That special season is upon us and is near to us in the same manner as the kingdom, fully present but not fully apprehended.

"The time has come, the Walrus said, to talk of many things" (or so wrote Lewis Carroll). That may be, but we are not always aware that the time is upon us. That is the difference between the disciples of Jesus and the disciples of other teachers in the ancient world. In that era, if you were recognized as a great teacher, students would come to you and ask permission to sit at your feet. Jesus did not wait for his disciples to come to him. He knew there were things lacking in their lives even though they themselves thought they were self-sufficient, able businessmen who did not need anything else. But the time was ripe for Jesus to interrupt their lives with eternal concerns. And his touch called for a response.

Even though these individuals would prove during the course of the gospel to be less than apt pupils, they responded, dropping everything to follow Jesus. We are called as well to respond, even though there are people much more qualified than we are for the work of the kingdom.

Who did Jesus get on this first fishing expedition? Peter, James, and John, his inner circle (but not his closest friends), who would be with him at the transfiguration but who would not be able to stay awake in Gethsemane. Throw in Andrew, who in other accounts made his share of cameo appearances, and count it a fairly good catch for a first toss of the net.

In addition to God's affirmation and the Son's response, Mark recorded the Spirit's consistent and constant action—often unseen, but apparent afterward, just as the movement of branches affirms the passage of the wind. The descent of the Spirit upon Jesus was a significant event. It marked the beginning of his ministry and confirmed the power present in him. This Spirit is all pervasive. It was present at the creation, brooding over the waters. It is the guider and shaper and mover throughout Scripture.

Some people limit the Spirit's presence to mystical, ecstatic events. In truth, however, the Spirit is manifest in many ordinary ways as well. The same Spirit that gave Jesus strength, even unto the cross, also gives courage to those who change diapers in nursing homes, who cook in soup kitchens, who minister to those with AIDS. This Spirit draws the empty soul to the Psalms, and even to the back pew of a church.

I remember one evening staring at the sky, thinking how odd the clouds looked. A few moments later I realized I was seeing the northern lights for the first time. I called the family and, with the mobile phone, called others to take a look. Despite the fact that it was a chilly night, there was no choice but to watch, because we cannot pick a time and place to view the aurora borealis. The call of the gospel is like that. We do not pick the moment. It picks us. We respond yea or nay.

Discussion and Action

1. What do you know about Jesus from the twenty brief verses that begin Mark's gospel?
2. Jesus heard himself called "My Son, the beloved," and the Spirit descended upon him at his time of baptism. Recall your own baptism experience. What word did you hear? What did it mean for you?
3. Was there a moment when God called you? If not God, then how about a member of your faith community? Tell about a time you were called.
4. What is your ministry? Is it something the rest of the church recognizes? Name the ministries of the people in your covenant group. How do they differ?

5. Why was it necessary for Jesus to experience time in the wilderness? Define your own wilderness time. When did you experience the most alienation from God, from people, from yourself? How did it end, if it has?

6. The arrest of John the Immerser ended one aspect of his ministry, although it made it possible for him to deal directly with Herod. Our own ministries change over time. What reluctance have you experienced when one chapter in your life in the church has closed? What doors, if any, opened up later?

7. Jesus called us to repentance. From what does our world, our church, and each person need to repent?

8. Close with prayers of repentance or the hymn "Here I Am Lord."

3

We've Never Seen Anything Like This
Mark 1:21—3:6

Jesus tries to keep his true identity hidden. His coming is not to be kept a secret permanently. It was a fact that had to be revealed in stages. The miracles begin to tell us more and more about the Son of God.

Personal Preparation

1. Read Mark 1:21—3:6. This section contains Jesus' miracles of healing. Some Christians practice anointing for healing, believing healing takes place in several ways: miraculously through the power of the Spirit, through hard work and the hands of human healers, and emotionally through the peace that allows us to bear trials. Reflect upon examples of healing you have experienced and be prepared to share these.

2. Has there been a person "possessed" by physical, emotional, or developmental problems who has claimed your time and energy, perhaps even to the point of exhaustion? What healing might be possible for that person? What healing is possible for you as you continue to work with this person?

3. Reflect on some secret in your life. You will not be asked to share secrets with the group. Instead, speak to God about these things.

4. When you are learning to know someone, what do you reveal about yourself at first? What do you keep "secret" until later? Why?

Understanding

Back at the dawn of the computer age, programmers were math cowboys or cowgirls who did miracles with yellow punch tape and hexadecimal code. My friend Ralph worked for computer firms from the time he was in high school. He made his way through college working on computers.

At the college Ralph attended, there was a math professor who disliked computer jockeys because they made money at what he considered a technology rather than a science. About a month before Ralph was to graduate, the professor made an ultimatum—take a math course or don't graduate. The professor implied that without the authority of a diploma, Ralph would not be able to work. In fact, Ralph did not graduate, but he made good money without a diploma (which he picked up many years later).

Jesus did not jump through anybody else's hoops either. No outsider told him what to do or gave him authority to perform the mighty works and wonders that appear in these chapters. When he entered the synagogue in Capernaum, "they were astounded at his teaching, for he taught them as one having authority, and not as the scribes." (1:22) Here was a person without a "diploma" who, nevertheless, seemed to be able to teach as well as any trained religious leader.

Who said Jesus could do this stuff? He did. The miracles of Jesus are an essential element of Mark's narrative. They demonstrate that there are no boundaries to God's kingdom. The natural and supernatural are part of one realm, and Jesus is Lord over all of it.

In this brief section, a man with an unclean spirit, Simon's mother-in-law, a leper, a paralytic, and many others are all healed. C.S. Lewis, in his book *Miracles*, is at pains to point out that the miracles of Jesus are not part of a sideshow. Strange and unnatural things, such as the turning of stones into bread, are not performed by Jesus. According to Lewis, the miraculous healings demonstrate through Jesus what the kingdom of God looks like. There is a reversal, a restoration, for those who have been cut off from the mainstream because of their illnesses or conditions. More than anything else, these healings demonstrate that the love of God is made real in action.

The first recorded healing in Mark is that of a demoniac. We may not have experience with an individual possessed by a demon, but this story makes it clear that Christ's authority is over all the realms and powers. It was the intention of this demon to demonstrate its own authority by disrupting worship in the synagogue. The demon's great question, "What have you to do with us, Jesus of Nazareth? Have you come to destroy us? I know who you are, the Holy One of God," drew clear battle lines. (1:24) By naming Jesus, the demon hoped to conjure and control him. But Jesus is not subject to the laws of nature. He has created them and, therefore, stands apart from them.

Whether you believe these individuals were possessed by evil or were suffering from mental illness, the effect is the same for the families whose lives are dominated by a mentally ill person. Fortunes can be spent on healing, to no avail. Families despair, but God's love is stronger than the evil that seems to rule our lives. God's authority will become apparent, now or later. These stories of healing are designed to give hope to the hopeless through faith in Jesus.

When the demon identified Jesus as the "Holy One of God," Mark tells us that "Jesus yelled at him, 'Shut up and get out of him!' " (1:25 Scholars' Version) This was Mark's first use of the Messianic Secret, spoken about in an earlier chapter. Three times in this section, in the stories of the exorcisms, Jesus demanded silence with regard to his identity.

The arrival of the Messiah was not a secret to be permanently hidden, but a fact that had to be revealed in stages. Anyone who makes a guess as to the identity of Jesus based solely on his wonder-works and teachings will have a skewed perception. Jesus is more than a miracle worker.

The sheer breadth of the healing in this section is impressive. In addition to the exorcisms, Jesus healed a leper, a social outcast whose disease made him unfit for human company. Part of the healing process included touching this untouchable man. We hardly need to mention the parallel situation with AIDS victims in our day.

It is hard to say which of the two latter healings is more impressive—the healing of the paralytic, something beyond the power of modern medicine, or the healing of Levi, a social outcast of another sort. Both healings prompted outrage: the first, because of the Savior's claim to be able to forgive sins, and the second, because no one wanted to deal with a no-account tax collector who had been freed from all labels and had become a person.

The authorities confronted Jesus with basic questions about the nature of his teachings. The fact that his ministry took him among the outcast and unclean was justified by his statement, "Those who are well have no need of a physician, but those who are sick; I have come to call not the righteous but sinners." (2:17) And because Jesus and his disciples ate and drank well, in direct contrast to the ascetic conduct of John the Immerser and his disciples, there was some question about the legitimacy of Jesus and his ministry. His reply was that as the arrival of the bridegroom at the house of the bride signaled the beginning of feasting, so too his arrival was the first sign of a new age. God's kingdom is fun.

The kingdom of God is too great to be bound by the old rules. Hence the saying, "No one puts new wine into old wineskins." (2:22) In those days, part of the fermenting process took place after the wine had been placed in the leather wineskin. The bubbles stretched the leather to its limit. To put new wine in an old wineskin would cause it to burst.

The life of the kingdom will burst the old wineskins of our former life. The joy cannot be contained within the bounds of our unhappiness. If we insist on trying to graft the new life onto old habits, we will succeed only in tearing the fabric of our lives.

Yet the most radical element of this new wine is a return to fundamentals. Jesus challenged the slavery of the sabbath and called for a return to its original intent, which was to benefit humanity. It is apparent from a reading of the gospels that sabbath activity was monitored. Working was not allowed on that holy day. The definition of work was exact, even to the number of steps one was allowed to take.

Jesus demanded that the people return to the original intent of the holiday. The sabbath was mandated in Exodus for the express purpose of providing rest for all people, both the chosen of God and the strangers among them. "The sabbath was made for humankind, and not humankind for the sabbath," Jesus proclaimed boldly, and then proclaimed himself Lord of the` sabbath. (2:27)

Prior to healing a man with a withered hand, Jesus challenged the religious authorities by asking, "Is it lawful to do good or to do harm on the sabbath, to save life or to kill?" (3:4) The Pharisees got the point. They also decided to get even. Despite the fact that they were religious leaders of the people, they united with the Herodians (court followers) to oppose Jesus. Their intent was to kill him.

Nowadays the merry-go-round never stops. Sometimes we get so exhausted we think we have to get away from things. Unfortunately, even when we are successful in carving out time for a vacation, the world keeps on going. This is one of the things I hate about going away. I never know what will greet me when I get back. Will there be a surprise bill in the mail? Did I get a letter that needed answering while I was gone? Was there an emergency at the church? Is the house okay?

This was true for Jesus as well. When he went to the home of Simon's mother-in-law, it was no doubt with rest and some down-home cooking in mind, but his hostess needed healing. (1:29-31) After that, even more people came for healing, and Jesus worked late into the night.

Despite the fact that the work never seemed to end for Jesus, he carved out time for private prayer and devotion. Rest. Retreat. Renewal. Not a way of life, but the definition of the sabbath. For some it might mean reading a book. For others it means working in the garden or mowing a lawn. However you define sabbath, one thing is sure. None of us has time for it and all of us need it.

Jesus showed us the way to practice the sabbath. As the hymn "Sweet Are the Promises" puts it, "He the great example is, and pattern for me."

Discussion and Action

1. Talk about any experiences of anointing for healing you have had. Share other healing-related stories from your life or your family's life.

2. Jesus wanted to keep his true identity a secret for a while, so that people would not make judgments before they knew the whole story—sort of a surprise party. Is

it possible for others to know you in part? Is it possible
to know the gospel in part?

3. How was the sabbath observed when you were
younger? What restrictions were placed upon behavior? How does that compare with how you observe the
sabbath now?

4. What forms of expression are part of your worship, both
personal and corporate? How do you address God? Do
you pray silently? out loud? in what posture? Does
anyone holler "Amen"? Do people applaud? What
instruments are allowed? Is there an opportunity to
share joys and concerns? What is the dress code?

5. How or where do you find time for the sabbath between
many demands and many people in your life? As a
group make plans for sabbath time this week.

6. Work with a member of your group, your congregation,
or a local association for the disabled to learn about the
difficulties faced by people with handicaps. For a few
minutes, experience what they experience. Blindfold
one person, plug the ears of someone else, have someone wear an oversized shirt without putting their arms
in the sleeves. How can your group or your congregation help to alleviate such difficulties for other church
members or visitors?

7. Consider an action response to your Bible study. Is
there a person or family dealing with illness, mental or
physical, with whom you can walk? How can you accompany or advocate for those who experience handicaps?

4

Who Then Is This?

Mark 3:7—4:41

*The parables reveal more and more about Jesus. But
even the disciples don't always grasp their significance.
We, like the disciples, must learn patience. Meaning
and understanding emerge with time.*

Personal Preparation

1. Read Mark 3:7—4:41. The parables of Jesus are so
   familiar we hardly hear what they are saying anymore.
   Look for and write in a brief phrase the meaning of each
   of these parables. Plan to take this to your group.
2. Pay special attention to what is commonly referred to
   as the parable of the sower. (4:1-9) Notice it is really
   not about the sower, but the seeds. How are you like
   the sower in the story? How are you like the seeds?
3. Write a parable that speaks directly to your life.

Understanding

During my years at Azusa High School, I was one of the
outsiders. My friends and I did not belong to any of the status
groups. Fortunately, we had each other. We were so far outside
we became insiders of sorts.

Others grew curious about us and sometimes sat near us at
lunch, straining to hear our jokes. If they got too close, we would
play a cruel trick. We would act as if we had been telling a joke,

and one of us would give the punch line, "So the one duck said to the other, 'Not the soap, the radio!' " We'd all break up in laughter and so would the intruder, who was so worried about not getting the joke he or she laughed even though no joke had been made.

All of us want to be in on the joke. It is difficult to look at a cartoon and then have to turn to someone and say, "I don't get it." But the disciples did not get it—the parables, that is. Jesus said, "You don't get this parable, so how are you going to understand other parables?" (4:13 Scholars' Version)

This may be encouraging. Jesus did not pick the best and the brightest for his inner circle. He picked people like us. Life's puzzles floor us. We ask ourselves what it is all about. That's good! We are not so far from the kingdom as we thought.

These parables of the kingdom are not that difficult. The parable of the seeds makes it clear that those who hear the word are not always on an equal footing, but if they receive the word of God, they will bear fruit a hundredfold. It also assures us that much of life is out of our control. The sower did little or nothing. God and the seeds did all the work. But the harvest was there.

The story about the lamp under the bushel basket reminds us to let our light shine in the world. The mustard seed story warns us not to judge a book by its cover. These are not tough stories, but the disciples asked what they meant. They were like us in our frustration and confusion. Why did Jesus pick them anyway? Why these twelve, and not better souls?

A few years ago I tried out for a part in *Man of La Mancha*, a musical about the life of Miguel de Cervantes. When I came home from the auditions, I told my wife Jennie I would be happy with any part except one of the muleteers, who are the scum of the earth.

Needless to say, I was cast as Pedro, the leader of the muleteers. But that is par for the course. I am always cast as the bad guy. It really does not bother me, though. One thing I have learned from theater is that we do not always get the part we want, and the best actors do not always get the biggest parts. We get the part we fit. Once chosen, there seems to be a logic to it all, so that by the time the show opens, I cannot imagine playing another role.

The Twelve were chosen because they fit the role God assigned them, just as we are chosen for our role in the faith. This does not mean we have no free will, no say in the matter. We choose to serve. God knows, and the community must discern, our best part. The parables illustrate the power of story. They are memorable because they are so true to life. It is helpful to think of them as anecdotes that had a point, bringing smiles, and perhaps even laughter to the listener. And remember, most of the original hearers got it without an explanation. For those of us who do not get it, who are still struggling with the gospel, the apostles in the narrative bring us hope in the face of our discouragement. God is going to give us a little more time.

Jesus continued to silence the demons in this section, even as he cast them out, because he wanted people to learn that the Son of God was not just a healer. These exorcisms led to new controversy. Scribes from Jerusalem come to town with a ridiculous accusation. The reason, they stated, that Jesus could cast out demons was that he called upon the prince of demons to help him. It was one of those simplistic arguments that sound reasonable until you take them apart. In this case, Jesus reminded his listeners that if there was that much infighting among the forces of evil, it was time to declare the Jubilee. He challenged them to consider that "no one can enter a strong man's house and plunder his property without first tying up the strong man." (3:27) Jesus was the one strong enough to overpower the "strong man," the adversary, whose rule over this world is strictly temporary.

Jesus then alluded to what is known as the "unforgivable sin." There has been a lot of speculation about what the unforgivable sin may be. Radio storyteller Garrison Keillor told a tale about a man in his hometown who claimed to have committed the unforgivable sin. It gave the man a certain aura, a gloomy glamour. He had been as bad as he could be and could not get any worse.

The whole business would be funny except that the unlikeliest souls fall into the depths of depression, convinced that they are guilty of this nameless sin. Usually, good folks have this belief, as if God has nothing better to do but damn them for the one indiscretion of their lives.

The unforgivable sin, to my mind, is really quite simple. It is failing to ask for forgiveness. It implies either that you do not recognize that you are a sinner, or that you have made the decision that your state is beyond hope. In other words, God can forgive anything, as long as we ask. But we have got to ask. The scribes did not ask.

The other controversy may hit closer to home. When Jesus went home, it was to find that the crowds had grown so great "they could not even eat." (3:20) That may not sound like a big deal to us, but in many places in the Middle East, eating together is one of the major events and hospitality is a sacred duty. Unexpected guests were good news and extra mouths to feed a cause for happiness. But with all the crowds around, they could not practice hospitality the way they wanted.

3:31-35

When the family of Jesus heard about all the fuss, they decided, "He has gone out of his mind," and set out to restrain him. (3:21) When Jesus was told that his mother and brothers were outside asking for him, he replied, "Who are my mother and my brothers?" (3:33) He then redefined the family to include all those who willingly join the covenant circle, who do "the will of God." (3:35) Which sounds good until you think about the hurt feelings that must have resulted from this statement, however true.

The Scriptures do not recognize family ties as the ultimate or most sacred of bonds, even while honoring them. I remember an adoption controversy in which the birth father claimed custody during his daughter's teen years because "blood is thicker than water." The young woman's real mother (distinct from her birth mother) became so confused she began to wonder if his statement was true. Once things were sorted out, however, mother and daughter realized that love and choice create the strongest bonds.

We are called into a family that recognizes God as parent. We gain this parent by choice, not inheritance. God has no grandchildren. We are all directly born of God's desire.

Although it is not an ideal situation, there may arise circumstances in which family must come second to God. The trick is not to fool ourselves and somehow mistakenly place our own desires in the second or first spot under the guise of serving God.

The final story in this section is the most important, and it brings into play all the latent fears of a generation without control. In the first chapter of Genesis, God separated land from water and subdued the primeval chaos, forever holding it in check. Even though this was a tenet of belief for God's people, it was hard to believe sometimes. Maybe this would be the year, they might have wondered, when the days would continue to grow shorter without a solstice to turn the tide. Maybe this storm would finally signal the triumph of chaos, when the greedy waters reclaimed all the territory marked out by God.

The story of Jesus calming the sea may have reminded his followers of the Jonah story. For many people today the Jonah story is an amusing fish tale for kids to enjoy. For the first Christians, it was a favorite subject for art. In his book *Ante Pacem*, Graydon Snyder declares that the Jonah story was depicted more often than any other scriptural theme in the first three centuries of Christian art.

And no wonder. Jonah, despite his sin, was carried through the primordial waters and brought to safety. Early Christians understood the waters of baptism to work in the same way, preserving them through life's stormy seas.

Jesus, like Jonah, was preserved through the storm, and with him the disciples who in their fear despaired of their lives. The difference, however, is that Jesus was blameless and rescued himself.

Put yourself in the place of the disciples. What would be more frightening, the storm or the fact that Jesus could control it? It is obvious that up until now the disciples did not get it. They did not know who Jesus was. The storm suddenly threw them off their moorings. They panicked. And panic is blind.

The disciples were still blind as they asked the question in awe and wonder, "Who then is this, that even the wind and the sea obey him?" (4:41)

Who indeed?

Discussion and Action

1. Share the meanings you find in the parables for this session. Share also any parables you wrote that speak to your life.

2. Based solely on the incidents in this section, who would you say Jesus is? How have you described Jesus to others at different points in your life? Today, how would you answer the question, Who then is this?

3. When have you, like the disciples, wanted more explanation in order to understand the parables, the gospel, and Jesus? Does your group or congregation encourage questions and religious searching?

4. Has there ever been a time when you had to place other considerations second in order to put God first? Did you meet with understanding, resentment, or confusion? How can you realistically test the Spirit in such a situation?

5. Have you ever felt as the disciples in the storm that God was somehow asleep and unaware of your pain? What do you do when God seems so absent?

6. Discuss setting up a telephone or prayer chain so members of the group can support each other. Can you do this so it includes more than your own group—perhaps the whole congregation?

5

Do You Not Yet Understand?
Mark 5:1—8:21

Despite the miracles, the people closest to Jesus still do not catch on. Sometimes it is the same for us. The closer we stand to something, the less we are able to see it whole and understand it.

Personal Preparation

1. Read Mark 5:1—8:21. Make a list of the various stories. Is there a common thread or connection?
2. What is the largest group you have ever prepared for or cooked for? What were your feelings when your guests arrived? What is your worst fear as a host?
3. Place yourself in the shoes of someone who lived near the madman in Mark 5:1-20. How would his madness have affected your life? What changes would you make to live with an insane person? What adjustments would you have to make when he was cured? Would you be able to accept and trust a person healed from insanity?

Understanding

It happens every year.

Late in the summer our family has made it a habit to host our entire church for dinner. We call it the Fiesta, and it involves making Mexican food for around a hundred and fifty people. In addition to church members, we invite friends from the theater, other writers, and co-workers from outside employment. In other words, we invite people from all the various circles in which we travel.

After a decade we have a system down pat. It involves purchasing, preparing, and decorating. There are the last frantic hours while all the Mexican food is set into place, and then the feeding frenzy follows. It's all great fun.

But every year I panic. What if there's not enough food? There always is, but I feed this particular anxiety by making more Spanish rice. It is ridiculous, I know, but out come the spices, tomato sauce, peppers, and, of course, the bags of rice. Like clockwork, every forty minutes or so I start another batch. Of course, there is too much Spanish rice. I end up defrosting the leftovers well past Christmas.

But no one wants to run out of food during a feed. That is why there is such an abundance at church potlucks. Members have a tendency to bring two or three dishes, just so "we don't run out." No one can recall a time when we ran out in living memory, but that does not quell the fears.

And fear it was that the disciples must have felt when they were confronted by the prospect of feeding over five thousand people. Who knows how much rice I would have cooked, faced with such a prospect?

There are two feedings in this sequence. The first took place among the Jews. The second happened in gentile territory. Although there are obvious parallels, there are significant differences. The disciples were far more panicked at the first feeding. Their impulse was to send everyone away. This was not as callous as it sounds. Middle Eastern hospitality ensured that all strangers would be taken in, fed, and lodged. How could they ever feed them all?

But Jesus saw the people as "sheep without a shepherd," calling to mind the language of Moses in Numbers 27:17. (6:34) Indeed, in the story there are parallels to the Greek version of the Exodus. The people needed to be released not from the foreign oppressor, but from the slavery of sin. The miraculous feeding calls to mind the doubt of the Israelites in the wilderness and the manna that sustained God's children in the desert for forty years.

One overlooked aspect of the miracle is that no one other than the disciples and Jesus knew what went on. The five thousand plus were seated while Jesus blessed the loaves and handed them to the disciples to distribute. Many of God's miracles take place out of our sight.

The incident looks ahead to the time of abundance that will come to pass when God's kingdom is fully realized, a time, in the words of the prophet Micah, when "they shall all sit under their own vines and under their own fig trees, and no one shall make them afraid." (Micah 4:4) The fact is, there is enough food and more to go around. Kingdom living could make this happen.

This first miraculous feeding occurred in the middle of a series of incidents in which Jesus was either not recognized or rejected. "Who then is this?" asked the disciples after the stilling of the storm. (4:41) Jesus was rejected in his home town. He was laughed at when he said, "The child is not dead, but sleeping." (5:39) The Pharisees accused him of failing to obey the laws about cleanliness.

In contrast, Jesus was recognized as Lord when he slipped into gentile territory. According to the late Bible scholar Robert Guelich, the second feeding, known as the "Feeding of the Four Thousand," occurred on the east side of the Sea of Galilee, a fact suggested by the movement to the western shore where Jesus was confronted by Jewish authorities. The setting of the story of the Syrophoenician woman, a Gentile who asked for her child's health, and the story of the deaf man who was healed, which come right before the second feeding story, also took place in gentile territory.

In the story of the Syrophoenician woman Jesus articulated the racism of his contemporaries. In response to the request from the woman that her non-Israelite child be healed, Jesus replied, "Let the children be fed first, for it is not fair to take the children's food and throw it to the dogs." (7:27) Dogs, which Jesus seems to have used as a term for non-Jews, were despised animals in the Middle East—scrawny little scavengers. I believe Jesus spoke these words to show his disciples just how ugly their own attitudes were.

Not long ago I was out driving when I spotted a bumper sticker just as ugly. "Fix America First!" it proclaimed. It expresses a common attitude that our country of origin is somehow isolated from the rest of the world. Those who express such sentiments define America too narrowly, in my experience. They often do not include individuals of differing economic or racial backgrounds, even if they are citizens of the United States.

The unnamed woman replied, "Sir, even the dogs under the table eat the children's crumbs." (7:28) God invites tough dialogue. Far from being satisfied with things as they were, Mark seemed to encourage his readers to question situations of injustice.

Jesus responded by healing the woman's daughter, granting a cure to a deaf man, and, in an act of literally sharing the crumbs from the children's dinner, feeding the four thousand who listened to him in gentile territory.

There are differences between the two tales. Rather than lift his eyes to heaven and send his blessing (a Jewish custom he performed in the first feeding), Jesus blessed the food itself (a gentile custom) in the second feeding. While he lamented that his own people were like sheep without a shepherd, he felt compassion for the Gentiles because of their physical needs. The first feeding was followed by a sign (walking on the water), which his disciples did not understand. The second feeding was followed by a demand for a sign from the religious authorities, which resulted in a heartfelt sigh of despair and the assurance that there would be no sign.

There is also a non-miracle in this section. "Now the disciples had forgotten to bring any bread; and they had only one loaf with them in the boat." (8:14) It almost seems as if the disciples were hinting, hoping for some more of that miraculous bread. "Do you not yet understand?" asked Jesus. (8:21) Look at how much was left over at each feeding, Jesus seems to have said. Don't you understand that God was at work there? And yet you still fuss over the fact that you have only one loaf.

We take our attention from the table to the grave, from the site of feasting to the solemnity of the tomb. Until modern history the grave was not a permanent resting place. After a generation or two, the bones were removed and someone else's remains were put in their place. As a result, the cemetery was not a particularly clean place in both senses of the word—literally and ritually.

A cemetery was the site of the story of the Gerasene demoniac. (5:1-20) This cemetery was a doubly unclean place for Jews because it was a gentile cemetery, enemy territory.

In this setting of decay lived a madman, the demoniac, who had plagued his neighbors beyond endurance. With the strength of someone under the influence of the drug PCP, he broke chains. No prison could hold him. With the persistence of a demon, he harmed himself. No person could tame him. Until now.

When Jesus arrived on the scene, the demoniac's first defense was to name Jesus. In this way he hoped to get the upper hand. When that did not work, he protested. "What have you to do with me, Jesus, Son of the Most High God?" (5:7) This was the defiant challenge of the demons inside. You are outside your home territory, Jesus. I am not one of God's people.

Most High God was the term used by pagans for Yahweh, the God of Israel. It recognized God's existence, but implied there were other gods as well. There is the suggestion in this question that the world was divided into spheres of influence. Israel's God would rule over some but not all of these.

This is one of the central questions in the Gospel of Mark. What has Jesus to do with any of us? Is he a teacher solely? Are his issues so tied up with the culture two thousand years ago that he has become an anachronism, an outdated, romantic notion? Can we put our allegiance to him in a pigeonhole, obeying where expedient, but recognizing that to be practical we cannot always follow his teachings?

The response of Jesus was to cast out the demon, known as Legion, without conjuring, without catchwords. But there was a cost. A whole herd of swine was lost. This in itself was frightening. More significant is the fact that the former demoniac was restored to personhood. He was no longer a cipher, but a human being who deserved to be in relationship with others. His fellow Gerasenes must learn to ignore the past and grow to know this person who had held them in sway through fear and terror. The demand for conquering love among us is sometimes the most frightening aspect of the gospel.

"I adjure you by God," said Legion at one point, "do not torment me." (5:7) This mirrors our own attitude toward our personal demons. "Don't cure me! I trust the demons I have more than the salvation I haven't seen." But Jesus did not negotiate. Even the bargain Legion made, to be transferred to the herd of pigs, led to the demon's destruction. We cannot both confront and excuse evil. Our own illnesses need to be confronted as well.

In marked contrast to the absolute power Jesus displayed over the spiritual and physical universe, he allowed people to accept or reject him without an attempt to force belief or adoration. Nowhere is this more evident than in what would have been for us the most painful event—rejection in the hometown. Many of us have left our homes to make a name for ourselves elsewhere, only to return and discover that what Jesus said is true. A prophet is without honor in his or her own country.

This powerlessness to force belief defines God's resolve to receive our love only if we freely offer it. There is nothing forced about our decision to proclaim Jesus as Lord.

To my mind the most important verse of Mark is 6:6, which reads: "Then he went about among the villages teaching." These few words probably represent the longest period of time expressed by any story in the gospel. The more words in a story, the shorter the duration in time it seems. The spectacular headlines in the gospel are reserved for bright moments. But the hard work of the kingdom, the stuff that calls for endurance and faithfulness, is so commonplace it is expressed very briefly.

This mirrors life. When we are involved in the cure of a demoniac, or when we are in the midst of a frantic feeding, the event requires many words and may bring us fame. But teaching Sunday school week after week, attending board or committee meetings, visiting shut-ins, saying daily prayers, studying the Bible—these things are briefly told, yet constitute the real work of the kingdom.

Who is this Jesus? Herod, representing worldly powers, heard of him but could not understand that here was something new. Since he considered himself the center of the universe, the only way he could make sense of what he heard about Jesus was to assume he must be John the Baptist all over again—John, who had been actively involved in Herod's life. The Pharisees heard about Jesus and attempted to force him into their categories of clean and unclean, prompting Jesus to ask once again, "Then do you also fail to understand?" (7:18) It is not what comes from without that imperils us, it is the evil within. Those in Nazareth, his hometown, could not take Jesus out of the context in which they knew him. "Is not this the carpenter, the son of Mary?" they asked, noting the names of his brothers and that his sisters lived among them. (6:3)

Contrast this with the outsiders, typified by the Syrophoenician woman whom Jesus addressed as "daughter." Is there a pattern emerging?

Discussion and Action

1. Talk about some of your experiences hosting or feeding guests, especially large groups of people.
2. Have you ever been part of a group that was hungry and needed food? Who are some of the people today needing to be fed, spiritually and/or physically?
3. It takes twenty-one pounds of grain to produce one pound of beef. Discuss or debate this question: In light of world hunger, is it moral to eat meat while others starve?
4. What qualifies to make someone a "Gerasene demoniac"? Beyond insanity, how about the disabled, those with Alzheimer's disease, alcoholics, hospice patients, the developmentally disabled, victims of violence or abusive relationships? Are there demons in these lives?
5. When is intervention necessary in cases like the above? Tell about cases of intervention or outsiders stepping in.
6. Is there someone in your group or church who lives with a "Gerasene demoniac"? Is there any way members of the group can gather to share the burden on a long-term, regular basis?

Leia

6

You Are the Messiah!
Mark 8:22—10:52

Finally, the disciples begin to understand. Thankfully, Jesus is patient, giving us all many chances to understand. And with understanding comes awesome responsibility.

Personal Preparation

1. Read Mark 8:22—10:52. If you are using your own Bible and want to mark it, highlight the sections in which Jesus talked about his upcoming death.
2. Think of occasions when someone has tried to talk to you about her or his approaching death. Did you downplay such talk and insist that things would be okay? Were you able to listen? Have you spoken to others about your death? This week, think of ways to talk openly about death with others.
3. Think about a time you thought you were being helpful to someone you loved, only to discover you actually hindered them. Did they rebuke you? If so, how did that make you feel? If not, how did you feel when you found out what you had done?

Understanding

I live in Indiana now. I used to live in California. I told my kids before we moved, "It's not better or worse. It's just different."

One of the differences, one of the few I do not enjoy, is that northern Indiana is flat. There is no place you can get high enough to really look around.

Back in Los Angeles, my running partner, Jerry Lear, and I used to jog steep hills in order to gain that thing we usually call a view, but which is really a perspective. When you get high enough, you see things a lot more clearly. My favorite spot was a hill I reached the hard way, running straight up the side of the hill to take me into the oil fields of Culver City. From there, an hour before sunrise, I could see the moon set in the San Fernando Mountains. On a clear morning I could see for forty miles or more. The traffic was already clogging the arteries of the city. To the west was Catalina, rising out of the ocean like a forgotten kingdom. To the north, south, and east were the towers of commerce, the sprawl of immigrants, and the desperation of South Central Los Angeles.

In her poem for the 1993 presidential inauguration, Maya Angelou wrote about the perspective you get from heights.

> But today, the Rock cries out to us, clearly, forcefully,
> Come, you may stand upon my
> Back and face your distant destiny...

One thing I have learned in Indiana, however, is that there is perspective to be gained at dirt level too. This city boy has become much more familiar with the difference between clay and sandy soils, the reason you can harvest corn in January, and how the water falls from the sky (something rarely observed in California) on the just and unjust alike.

The passage of Mark for this session focuses on perspective gained in flat land and on the heights. Both are crucial revelations. Here are real turning points in the gospel story.

The sequence begins with the strangest healing in Scripture, the blind man at Bethsaida. I am reminded of the time in Los Angeles when I was walking through the church grounds in the early evening. I paused a few feet from a familiar lamppost. There was something on the wall. A paint stain? A piece of cloth? A hat? My eyes were seeing something but my brain could not interpret it. I finally realized it was a moth, a gorgeous moth with an eight-inch wingspan. For the longest time, I

could see it, but I simply could not make it out. Sight came
before perception.

The incident reminds me of the cure of the blind man at
Bethsaida. When his eyes were first opened, he could not see
clearly. He could not recognize things for what they were. "I can
see people, but they look like trees, walking," he said. (8:24)
What was wrong? Was Jesus less capable of a miracle that day?
Hardly. Some things come in stages. Once again, first comes
sight, then perception.

The disciples were only seeing, not perceiving. They needed
more understanding to catch up with the outsiders who had
already figured out that Jesus is Lord.

This story gives us permission, as well, to give things a second
try. Writers know that a second draft is better than the first.
Most of us want to finish each task on the first go. But a "second
draft" offers us the hope that not only can the healing touch of
Jesus make us well, but if we are not yet well, Jesus may touch
us again.

What followed was a turning point in the Gospel of Mark.
Jesus and his disciples set out for the villages of Caesarea
Philippi. On the road he questioned the disciples, asking, "Who
do people say that I am?" (8:27)

Most of us remember that uncomfortable moment in school
when the teacher asked a question to which we *might* know the
answer. There was an awful silence while everyone tried to bore
holes through their desks with their eyes. No one met the
teacher's gaze. And you hoped against hope that someone
else would answer this question. Maybe the next one would
be easier.

When Jesus asked the $64,000 question, the disciples seemed
to hem and haw and only finally made halfhearted guesses.
Jesus, they suggested, might be one of the prophets, or Elijah,
or John the Baptist. Each of the guesses was safe, relying on
what had happened before. They tried to identify Jesus with
the past.

Then came the clincher: "But who do you say that I am?"
(8:19) Thank heaven for the rest of the disciples that Peter was
the kind of student who always pipes up, right answer or no.

"You are the Messiah."

Previously, only the outsiders understood about Jesus. Now an insider recognized Jesus for who he was. However, this answer was correct only if fully understood. So Jesus "sternly ordered them not to tell anyone about him. Then he began to teach them that the Son of Man must undergo great suffering, and be rejected by the elders, the chief priests, and the scribes, and be killed, and after three days rise again. He said all this quite openly." (8:30-32)

Not wishing to embarrass Jesus in front of the Apostles, Peter "took him aside and began to rebuke him." (8:32) This led to one of the harshest sayings of Jesus in the gospels, and it was directed against one of his own: "Get behind me, Satan!" (8:33)

How embarrassing and confusing it must have been for Peter and the others. The revelation that Jesus was the Messiah must have symbolized for them conquest and glory. Instead, their leader made it clear there was no triumph yet, not without the cross.

The idea that we must die to live seems alien in a world that prizes only success. Our comics and pundits routinely ridicule those athletic teams that have the misfortune to finish second. Last place means shame and unemployment. It is a central tenet of Christian faith that those who lead should truly be the greatest servants among the gathered. Indeed, real leadership has nothing to do with power as we usually think of it.

On three occasions Jesus would attempt to teach his disciples that the Son of Man must suffer many things. The phrase generally translated "Son of Man" is a title drawn directly from Hebrew Scriptures. The term could be translated "Son of Adam," or, as the New Revised Standard Version chose, "a human being."

Look at how Job uses this term. Job 25:4-6 paints a distressing picture of the plight of the Son of Man, or "human being": "How then can a mortal be righteous before God? How can one born of woman be pure? If even the moon is not bright and the stars are not pure in his sight, how much less a mortal, who is a maggot, and a human being, who is a worm!"

Contrast Job's view with the exalted status of the Son of Man in Psalm 8:3-5: "When I look at your heavens, the work of your fingers, the moon and the stars that you have established; what are human beings that you are mindful of them, mortals that you care for them? Yet you have made them a little lower than God, and crowned them with glory and honor."

The visions of Daniel equated the Son of Man with the Ancient of Days, or "Ancient One," who will be revealed as the Lord of Power when God's kingdom is established universally. "As I watched in the night visions, I saw one like a human being coming with the clouds of heaven. And he came to the Ancient One and was presented before him. To him was given dominion and glory and kingship, that all peoples, nations, and languages should serve him. His dominion is an everlasting dominion that shall not pass away, and his kingship is one that shall never be destroyed." (Daniel 7:13-14)

Which is the accurate portrait of the Son of Man? All of the above. The trouble is that the disciples only wanted to see the glory. They lacked perspective.

Jesus saw all too clearly where his path would lead. He could not bear to be distracted, not so close to the goal, not when it would have been so easy to turn aside. I remember many times while running distance races how well-meaning spectators would shout to us in our exhaustion, "You're almost there! Just around the corner!" It wasn't true. Maybe they thought they were encouraging us, but they just made it harder.

When Peter refused to hear about the cross, he unwittingly joined in the temptation of Jesus to take the easy path, to seek worldly glory instead of lasting redemption.

Things should have come into clearer focus for the disciples with the transfiguration. For a brief moment, the resurrected Lord was revealed to the disciples prior to the crucifixion.

When I was a kid, there was a rule at the "Rec. Center" that the older kids had to bat opposite their normal stance (lefties batted right-handed, and vice versa) in order to even things out. This made the game closer and was part of playing fair. The transfiguration shows that God played fair. The incarnation is not a story about a God who takes human form and drops it whenever it is convenient. He does not run into a telephone booth and change costumes when things get tough. The transfiguration shows that Jesus could have knocked heads together any time he wished. The power and the glory evident in the resurrection were implicit all along, but they were veiled. God plays fair.With Jesus were Moses and Elijah. I have to assume there were no portraits available, yet the disciples knew who they were without being told. This tells me that in the kingdom, those things we now know in part we shall know in full. The pair, Moses and Elijah, represented the Law and the Prophets, which are perfectly fulfilled in Jesus.

Like most of us, Peter sought to freeze-frame the moment, asking for permission to set up tents, monuments, souvenir stands, and a plaque that begins, "On this site in the year of Caesar." Like most of us, Peter wanted to stay on the mountaintop, but there was work to be done in the valley. What remains is the way of the cross. The light must be veiled a little longer

What are we to think of this majesty that appears in both the cross and the crown? If we truly comprehend the difficulty of the road, the cost of the trying and the dying, will we be able to take the first steps with Jesus toward glory?

This section offers two suggestions. First we are called to accept the gospel like a little child. I am a little leery of romanticizing children and childhood. As a veteran department store Santa, I know how wiggly and difficult little children can be, especially at Christmas time, and especially when Santa has to be nice! Pictures of the "suffer the little children to come unto me" event always look so placid and peaceful. I do not believe it. That is why I admire Jesus all the more for drawing the children into his life when he was so very tired.

Moreover, in the ancient world, as in many places in the world today, the sad fact is that children were second-class citizens who did not become valuable until they started earning cash for the family. They were expendable, at the bottom rung of society. But Jesus turned things upside down by putting children first.

We must put the downtrodden and the oppressed first, even though there is no money in it. And we must accept the gospel with the same uncritical belief a child brings to her or his life.

It is not easy. Not when the call comes to leave everything and follow him. The rich young man was not equal to the task. Peter, on behalf of the disciples, claimed they had left all. Nevertheless, we may ask with the disciples how anyone can be saved. This is the Good News, as Jesus answered, "For mortals

it is impossible, but not for God; for God all things are possible."
(10:27)
Our response is one with the father who desperately begged
for his child to be healed. He used the near fatal word "if" in his
request for help. "If you are able...," he prefaced his request.
(9:22) When Jesus answered that anything is possible for those
who believe, the man replied, "I believe; help my unbelief!"
(9:24)
If things are coming into focus, then perhaps you are ready
for the question Jesus asked to those who wanted to share in his
kingdom. "Jesus said to them, 'You do not know what you are
asking. Are you able to drink the cup that I drink, or be baptized
with the baptism that I am baptized with?' They replied, 'We
are able.' " (10:38-39)
Are you?

Discussion and Action

1. Sing "Are Ye Able." If you are not singers, let each
   individual read a line in turn and then share the chorus
   together. Or have several people sing the questions,
   then all sing the chorus response.
2. What is the hardest thing you face this week? How can
   others aid you in this task? Are there some things you
   must face alone?
3. This week's lesson centers on the Messiah's insistence
   that he must be crucified in order to rise. The personal
   preparation for this session invited you to reflect on
   times you may have downplayed someone else's reflection on his or her own death. Talk about death as a
   group. Give the gift of your attention.
4. The real Jesus was revealed in the transfiguration.
   Reveal something about yourself that gives a clearer
   picture of who you are, perhaps some dream for the
   future, some call to ministry with which you struggle,
   some hobby that is especially fulfilling for you.
5. Discuss your response to Jesus' questions. Can you
   accept a suffering Savior?

7

By What Authority?
Mark 11:1—12:44

Instead of hiding his authority and power, Jesus begins to assert it so that all will know his true mission. But no one says it better than the widow with her mite.

Personal Preparation

1. Read Mark 11:1—12:44. The section begins with Jesus' triumphant entry into Jerusalem and ends with the story of the widow's mite. When, if ever, have you received recognition for what you did, deserved or otherwise? Was there a time you gave your all, as the widow, for which you received no recognition?
2. Was there ever an occasion when you were called upon to take charge of things? Was it unexpected? Did you have any warning? Was your authority challenged?
3. Is it difficult for you to accept someone else's authority? Do you demand proof when someone tells you something? What sort of proof suffices for you?

Understanding

They say the ground gave too willingly a year after the Battle of Gettysburg. Too many bodies buried too quickly in graves too shallow by half. The odor of decay could not be masked by the flowers that fed on the corruption beneath.

The place had been prettied for decades when I first came there in 1974. I had been traveling around the country with a group of fellow college students, performing a play about our church heritage. Some of us took a side trip to the battlefield to take a look around.

I remember nearly swooning at the site of Pickett's Charge. The thought of standing on the same ground where over thirteen thousand men began a walk toward their doom was sobering, and a little sickening. The grass was too green, the sun too bright, the flowers too yellow, the sky too blue, for a scene of such destruction.

We had been told at the start of our tour that the place was the high-water mark of the Confederacy. The thing about a high-water mark, that point at which we can say "This is as good as it gets," is that we usually do not know until later that that was as good as it would get. I believe, for instance, that as a runner I have run my fastest races. But that is only from the perspective of several years. At the time I ran my best 5K, 10K, and marathon, I thought I might still have a faster run in me.

Appearances are deceiving. The downward decline sneaks up on us. Only later is it apparent that we have peaked.

The eleventh verse of the eleventh chapter of the gospel records the high-water mark of the earthly ministry of Jesus. "Then he entered Jerusalem and went into the temple; and when he had looked around at everything, as it was already late, he went out to Bethany with the twelve."

On one side of this verse is the triumphant entry into Jerusalem. Jesus laid claim to someone else's colt and entered the holy city. People along the way shouted his royal title (for which he would soon be executed), the Son of David.

On the other side is an unremitting challenge to his ministry by the authorities, who sought first to discredit, then kill him. But, oh, the golden moment. The sun as it set transformed every tile, every block of marble, as if etching anew with shadow every crack and line. Jesus stood in the Temple and took a look around. Then back to Bethany, back to friends, the tide ebbed and receded, and night fell.

It was the people who recognized, seemingly without cue, that Jesus was Lord. But his authority is challenged by others, and this challenge defines this section of Scripture.

The messianic secret was now out. There was no need to hide anymore, because Jesus was about to be revealed, both as the crucified and the risen Lord. In this section he asserted his authority three times, and his assertions were countered by three challenges. His assertions were public. By contrast, the challenges of others were marked by subterfuge and deceit.

Jesus first asserted his authority over the people and the city in his triumphant entry. As if born for the kingdom, he took ownership of the colt. Instead of denying or hiding his role, he accepted the accolades of the people.

On the following day, he asserted his power over nature by making a fig tree wither on demand. The tree's close proximity to Jerusalem, the supposed seat of religious authority, gave this curse added significance. Moreover, the fact that he delivered a curse at all confirmed that he had the power of judgment and that there are winners and losers.

His final assertion of authority drew lines that presented a challenge to the powers and principalities. When Jesus entered the Temple, he used his authority over the Temple and the economy by overturning the tables of the money changers and driving out those who were conducting business there.

When people began the practice of selling animals for sacrifice and changing money in the Temple, it was probably intended as a service for those who had to travel on foot for two or three days in order to worship there. The problem of making a long, hard journey without blemishing the sacrificial animals was alleviated by purchasing the appropriate creature on site. Then there was the problem of currency to pay Temple taxes. The empire's money, with its imprint of the emperor, was forbidden in the Temple and had to be exchanged in the outer courtyard for locally minted money.

As time went by, this practice evolved into a way to gouge those who had no real choice. Not unlike the concessions sold at amusement parks and ball games, it was the only game in town. Prices and exchange rates could be exorbitant. Instead of a holy site, the Temple became a marketplace where entrepreneurs had much to gain and little to sacrifice.

Jesus not only felt anger at this misuse of the Temple, he showed it. Some believers are uncomfortable with this outward display. They wonder, aren't Christians supposed to be nice at all times? But there it is. Jesus not only got angry, he got good and angry.

Anger should not be confused with violence. One does not necessarily lead to the other. Anger is an appropriate response to oppression, greed, and institutional violence. Anger leads to action, and with God's help, it can be an appropriate action.

Some years ago, formula companies began to foist their products on Third World nations, convincing mothers that it was more modern to bypass breast milk and feed their children a canned formula. They gave out free samples, and once the mother's milk dried up, she was forced to buy formula. Because of the rampant poverty, many women diluted the formula with unclean water or substituted other fluids. The children suffered.

Anger led to boycotts against manufacturers who, under pressure, finally reversed their practices. Anger is an appropriate response, especially when it leads to positive action. But the action Jesus took inevitably made authorities in Jerusalem feel threatened. People do not take it kindly when you interfere with their pocketbooks. Ask any preacher who has had the courage to suggest how people should spend their cash. We are willing to share almost anything with the community, except access to our checkbooks. The response to the anger and action of Jesus was immediate: "And when the chief priests and the scribes heard it, they kept looking for a way to kill him; for they were afraid of him, because the whole crowd was spellbound by his teaching." (11:18)

So the challenges began on the third day. The chief priests, scribes, and elders represented a group that had found a way to accommodate the existing religious and political structures. They confronted Jesus with the questions, "By what authority are you doing these things? Who gave you this authority to do them?" (11:28)

Jesus turned the tables on his adversaries by asking them a loaded question. He would answer their questions if they would answer his, "Did the baptism of John come from heaven, or was it of human origin?" (11:29) Jesus' question was not a tough one, except that for the religious leaders there was no right answer—not because they did not have an opinion, but because they did not want to risk unpopularity. If they said John's authority came from God, then Jesus could ask them why they did not believe him. If their answer was that John's authority was of human origin, the crowd would turn against them. Round one for Jesus.

The second challenge came from the Pharisees. Because of occasions like this, their name has become a synonym for corruption. Actually, Pharisaic Judaism, with its belief in angels and the afterlife, would probably be the branch of first-century faith that would be most comfortable to modern Christians. Pharisees were the leaders of the party of the people. Their teachers were the rabbis in the synagogues. Teachers like Hillel and Gamaliel taught admirable doctrines. Unfortunately, the group is often judged by only a few.

Their trap was set in the form of a question laced with false flattery. "Teacher, we know that you are sincere, and show deference to no one," they began, and proceeded to ask if it was lawful to pay taxes to the emperor. (12:14) The strategy was simple. If Jesus answered yes, he would disillusion the people and alienate the revolutionaries. If he answered no, he was guilty of treason.

When Jesus asked them for a coin, it became clear that regardless of his answer, the Pharisees had already made their choice. Their coins bore the image of the Roman emperor. They would traffic with the occupying government. They had no wish to be enlightened by Jesus. They just wanted the people's choice to fail.

The final challenge came from the Sadducees, who did not believe in angels or an afterlife and accepted only the first five books of the Bible as canonical. They were part of the elite. Their challenge to Jesus was couched in terms of a *reductio ad absurdum*, a technique in which a person's beliefs are reduced to an absurdity.

Whenever religious dialogue is carried out through slogans, bumper stickers, and innuendo, you can be certain that there is no substance to the arguments. The Sadducees did not desire dialogue. Instead, they attempted to reduce the idea of resurrection to an absurdity by creating a ridiculous situation.

Judaism took from Leviticus what was known as the Levirite duty. In the event that a man died leaving a family without heirs, it was the duty of his brother to marry the widow for the purpose of bringing into the world children who would bear the deceased man's name. The Sadducees asked whose wife a woman would be who married seven brothers in turn, each brother dying before fathering children.

Some people just do not get it. The question does not make sense in the light of eternity. As Jesus said, "Is not this the reason you are wrong, that you know neither the scriptures nor the power of God?" (12:24) Trick questions do not destroy the faith. If you want the answer to questions like these you must walk together, dialogue together, in order to come to answers that makes sense to the community. As time went by, the Levirite duty was abandoned by God's people, to the point where it is illegal in Israel today.

In the midst of these challenges, Jesus told the parable of the vineyard. The religious leaders could hardly fail to see themselves as the tenants who forgot they did not own the vineyard and in turn rejected the master's servants, finally killing the master's son to protect what was never theirs.

In contrast to these three challenges came a scribe who recognized Jesus for who he really was. The scribe brings us back to a world in which Jesus is acclaimed by his supported. The scribe asked the sincere question, "Which commandment is the first of all?" (12:28)

The answer of Jesus was twofold. Rather than one commandment, he paired the *Shema* from Deuteronomy with a command from Leviticus. "Hear O Israel: the Lord is our God, the Lord alone" is still a part of Jewish worship today. (Deut. 6:4) Named the *Shema* after the first word in the prayer, the command to "Hear!" is one that Israel is called to cherish, writing it down at every chance and praying it daily. The reminder that the Lord our God is one and is to be loved with heart and mind and strength is paired with the Levitical command to love one's neighbor as oneself. (Lev. 19:18)

The scribe's sincerity was proved by his response: "You are right, Teacher." Jesus responded by telling the scribe that he was not far from the kingdom of God. There was hope for the people.

At the end of these controversies, the real show started. Words, words, words are what we have had so far. Now, finally, there is some action. The widow entered with her offering. You can talk all you want, but there are times you have to get off the bench and get into the ball game. Talk is cheap. God's work is being done around the world by people who sacrifice everything. No one knows the extent of their sacrifices, and they do not expect any reward or acclaim. Second-rate football announcers focus on the ball carrier and sometimes say things like, "He gained all that yardage by himself." Those who have played the game know nothing could be further from the truth. There are linemen with broken noses who open the holes for the ball carriers. A good analyst is quick to point out what the ten other guys were doing during a play.

Jesus knew how the real Temple operated. A big show was going on in front of everyone, but the real action took place when the widow walked in virtually unseen and put her precious two cents in the box.

Discussion and Action

1. Discuss your answers to the first question of personal preparation, regarding undeserved recognition or stellar deeds ignored.
2. What authority do you exercise in your everyday life? How did you come to be in that position?
3. How much authority should any person be allowed to have? What are the limits? Does this include the power of life and death, access to food, the right to bear children? How much authority does Jesus have in your life?
4. Make a list of the temptations offered by the worldly kingdom of the day. Which tempt you personally, and which do not affect you at all?
5. What does it mean to have a suffering Savior, when we live in the real world that expects only success?
6. In what situations do we prefer the "triumphal" to the "suffering" way? What is the meaning of suffering discipleship? How are we to empty ourselves?

8

Do Not Be Alarmed
Mark 13:1-37

*When Jesus spoke of the end time, when Daniel's story
and visions were shared, when John repeated what he
had been told from heaven, it was with the same aim
in view—to comfort.*

Personal Preparation

1. Think about the greatest watershed in your life. What
   event was so earthshaking, for good or ill, that you now
   identify everything in your life by whether it happened
   before or after that event?
2. Read Mark 13 aloud. How do these words make you
   feel?
3. How seriously do you take talk about the end of the
   world? Are you what I call a "calenderizer," trying to
   figure out the exact time of the end of the earth? Do
   you take this passage in Mark 13 to be a metaphor, or
   should it be taken literally? What does this passage say
   to your life?

Understanding

It was in the fifth grade that I finally realized God intended the
world to end someday.

The teacher who told us that the world would end thought
she was giving us good news, but we all reacted with alarm. Deep

within I thought, this is not fair. I had not done any living yet! While the teacher explained that the end of the world would be good because God's plan would be fulfilled, I prayed silently that God would hold off just a little while.

Yet every December this and similar scriptures were read as part of the lectionary. I always got a shiver of delight from hearing about the mysterious "abomination of desolation." It just never occurred to me this might become part of my real life.

Later, in high school, I read a commentary on the New Testament written by a professor of Greek mythology. She assured her readers that the gentle, kind Jesus could never have said anything harsh, including those awful words about the end of the world. Later interpolators, editors, and scribes must have added those verses, she said.

For a while, people thought that the original Christian faith was something full of sweetness and light, that somehow grouches like Paul came along later to make it a difficult religion. Well, now we all know better. It was Jesus who said the toughest things in the Bible. For the oppressed and downtrodden, there is comfort and the promise that the first shall be last. But for the powerful and aloof, there is warning, even condemnation.

For some people who focus on the end of the world, these verses are part of a great code that, though convoluted, reveals the exact sequence of the end of time. In my own lifetime, the date for the end has been set several times. Back when Secretary of State Henry Kissinger was supposedly the Antichrist (according to his enemies), the date for the end of the world was 1971, then '72, then '74. Once these years slipped by, the same writers without apology began to focus on the late seventies. The book *Eighty-eight Reasons the World Will End in 1988* was distributed to ministers across the country free of charge. Then the author had the nerve to follow it with a sequel twelve months later, explaining why he was off by one year.

There is a growing realization, however, that a calendar interpretation of apocalyptic literature is neither consistent with the intent of Scripture, nor in the least bit useful. Bible scholar Vernard Eller has made the cogent point in his book *Revelation: The Most Revealing Book of the Bible,* that everyone who has attempted to wring a date out of the apocalypses has failed.

What is the purpose of this literature? Is it to frighten us? Hardly. When Jesus spoke of the end time, when Daniel's story and visions were shared, when John repeated what he had been told from heaven, it was with the same aim in view—to comfort.

To those who are too comfortable in this world, it might be disconcerting to think about the end of luxury. But to a people under siege, the urgent message is, take comfort! Hold on just a little longer! Don't blink. You ain't seen nothing yet.

And "see" is the correct verb. Revelation, Daniel, and the apocalypse of Jesus are nothing less than the gospel in visual, or video, form.

Eller, in his book, gave the example of Picasso's "Guernica." The painting is not a photographic reproduction of the bombing it commemorates. The images are jumbled, a mish-mash of anguish and terror. The result, however, is greater clarity about the horror of innocent suffering and the cruelty of war.

In the same fashion, the images in an apocalypse are not parts of a photograph intended to scientifically reproduce the sensations of the end of the world. Instead, the intent is to show that "like a woman in labor, the mind has fantasies." (Sirach 34:5) The tremendous labor pains that accompany the birth of the new creation will result in events that cannot be described in temporal language. Metaphors and similes will have to do.

The images presented in Mark are no less striking than in the other examples of apocalypse: "But in those days, after that suffering, the sun will be darkened, and the moon will not give its light, and the stars will be falling from heaven, and the powers in the heavens will be shaken." (13:24-25) Mark's reminder that "they will see 'the Son of Man coming in clouds' with great power and glory," with its direct allusion to the vision of Daniel 7, tied the hopes of the old and new covenants together. (13:26)

One overwhelming factor must be kept in mind when examining the genre of apocalyptic literature: God is in charge. That the fulfillment of the kingdom will come suddenly determines the nature of our response. Be alert. If we knew when these things would happen, we would be like students who wait until the night before the test and cram weeks worth of study into a few precious hours. We must always be ready for God's kingdom.

Being ready does not, however, imply a retreat from the world. C.S. Lewis, in the title essay of the book *The World's Last Night*, likened the appropriate attitude to that of the anonymous First Servant in Shakespeare's play *King Lear*. This unnamed servant walks on stage when an atrocity is about to be committed by his master. Speaking barely eight lines, he tries to stop the blinding of an elderly man. The servant is killed.

"That is his whole part: eight lines all told," wrote Lewis. "But if it were real life and not a play, that is the part it would be best to have acted." That is because, as Lewis put it, when the inspector arrived we were found at our post.

A quick look at the apocalypse as recorded by Mark shows these words fit the pattern. From the Mount of Olives one could look down on the Temple, and it was on that spot that Peter, James, John, and Andrew asked Jesus, "Tell us, when will this be, and what will be the sign that all these things are about to be accomplished?" (13:4) Still fresh in their minds was their master's prediction that a time would come when not one stone would be left standing on another.

In strongly worded language, Jesus made it clear that the signs of the end could easily be mistaken for events that occur in every generation: "Beware that no one leads you astray. Many will come in my name and say, 'I am he!' and they will lead many astray. When you hear of wars and rumors of wars, do not be alarmed; this must take place, but the end is still to come. For nation will rise against nation, and kingdom against kingdom; there will be earthquakes in various places; there will be famines. This is but the beginning of the birthpangs." (13:5-8)

Moreover, the spread of the good news would entail personal risk for anyone involved. "As for yourselves, beware," is the way Jesus put it. (13:9) This was consistent with the stories in the Book of Daniel, and the appearance of the martyred in Revelation. But as shown by the martyrdom of Stephen and the persecution described throughout the Acts of the Apostles, rather than squelch the faith, these events aided the spread of Christ to the world.

Because God is in control, there will be restraint, even when it seems that everything is about to be destroyed. The words in Mark 13:20 ("And if the Lord had not cut short those days, no one would be saved; but for the sake of the elect, whom he chose, he has cut short those days") are reminiscent of Revelation 6:5-6. When the third seal was opened, and the black horse was loosed, John recorded, "I heard what seemed to be a voice in the midst of the four living creatures saying, 'A quart of wheat for a day's pay, and three quarts of barley for a day's pay, but do not damage the olive oil and the wine!' " Things will never get as bad as they might.

One thing is certain: "But about that day or hour no one knows, neither the angels in heaven, nor the Son, but only the Father." (13:32) This is a literal statement that many literalists ignore! Yet the proof of it is found in the words of Jesus: "Truly I tell you, this generation will not pass away until all these things have taken place." (13:30)

Again in *The World's Last Night,* C.S. Lewis pointed to this verse as the ultimate authority that Jesus was fully human. "It is certainly the most embarrassing verse in the Bible," Lewis wrote. It is not humiliating because Jesus said it, but because Jesus was wrong. The entire generation he addressed died without seeing the coming of the Lord on the clouds.

While admitting he could not explain the mechanics, Lewis asserted that the ignorance of Jesus on this issue proved that God did not cheat in the incarnation. While fully God and in control of the universe, he was also fully human and shared our weaknesses and failures.

If there is any clear sign when the end will come, it is alluded to in the statement: "But when you see the desolating sacrilege set up where it ought not to be (let the reader understand), then those in Judea must flee to the mountains." (13:14) That is of little help, however. The key words are variously translated by such terms as "the abomination of desolation" (the words that thrilled me as a child), the "devastating desecration" (Scholars' Version), and "abomination which causes desolation" (New International Version). These are taken directly from prophecies in Daniel 9:27 and 12:11 that were interpreted to refer to the horrifying desecration of the Temple, which occurred when Antiochus Epiphanus IV sacrificed an unclean animal to the god Zeus on the altar of the Judean Temple. (1 Macc. 1:54) What to the people was an unspeakable sacrilege was punished by God in the eyes of the people. Some, as recorded in the books of the Maccabees, took up arms to cast out the invaders. The viewpoint of Daniel, however, was that God's people, in waiting, would triumph through God's power and not their own. Mark's readers knew about the historical abomination of desolation. Rather than expect an exact repeat of the Temple sacrilege, they probably steeled themselves for another sacrilege beyond words. What this might be is anyone's guess. But we are surrounded by abominations in our violent world, and any one of them is a reminder of how desperately we need the fulfillment of God's kingdom.

And that is the real message of this chapter. It came after the authority of Jesus had been questioned by the religious leaders. It came before his betrayal and death.

What is left? Nothing but the promise that we cannot expect anything better. Nothing but the assurance that it is going to get worse before it gets better. Nothing but the certainty that this too shall pass, and a day is dawning when at the name of Jesus every knee shall bow, when God's sovereignty becomes obvious to all, when the kingdom we see through a glass darkly we will come to know face to face.

"Stay awake!" urged Jesus, because we do not and cannot know the moment. And rather than speculate on the ultimate destiny of those we hate, it would not hurt to do a little spiritual housecleaning. John Donne put it best in one of his Holy Sonnets, when he wrote:

At the round earth's imagined corners, blow
Your trumpets, Angels, and arise, arise
From death, you numberless infinities
Of souls, and to your scattered bodies go.
All whom the flood did, and fire shall o'erthrow,
All whom war, dearth, age, agues, tyrannies,
Despair, law, chance, hath slain, and you whose eyes
Shall behold God, and never taste death's woe.
But let them sleep, Lord, and me mourn a space
For, if above all these, my sins abound
'Tis late to ask abundance of thy grace
When we are there; here on this solid ground
Teach me how to repent; for that's as good
As if thou had sealed my pardon with thy blood.

Discussion and Action

1. Share the watershed events or experiences you named in your personal preparation.
2. Talk about your feelings as you read this little apocalypse.
3. Read Revelation 21:1-5 and 21:22—22:7, or if you have more time, all of Revelation 21 and 22. What message for life today do these apocalyptic scriptures speak?
4. When did you first become aware that the world would end? How did you personally feel at the time?
5. What qualifies as the "abomination of desolation" for you? Respond to each person's choice.
6. Share faith with each other. In the midst of suffering and despair and evil in the world, how do you keep the faith? Where is your hope?
7. Sing favorite hymns that give you hope.

9

Truly This Was God's Son
Mark 14:1—15:47

*Jesus died alone, denied, forsaken, and abandoned by
his disciples. But even in his death, faith began to grow.
After all it was a Gentile at the foot of the cross who
recognized Jesus and said "Truly this was God's Son."*

Personal Preparation

1. Take the time to read Mark 14 and 15 aloud. It will take
   a while. Reflect or pray quietly when you finish.
2. Write a short paragraph describing your feelings as one
   of the following individuals: the woman who anointed
   the feet of Jesus, the young man who fled naked from
   the scene, a disciple trying to stay awake in Gethsemane, Peter as he denied Jesus, Judas preparing to
   betray Jesus, a guard who helped crucify Jesus, or one
   of the women at the cross. Be prepared to share your
   paragraph.

Understanding

I turn our Easter sunrise service over to the Wednesday Club
students. Some read scripture or prayers or lead responsive
liturgies; others collect the offering or play special music. Some
preach. The sermons are short, self-written, and sharp. Their
perspective is quite different than mine, which is why I encourage the practice.

One year Steve Tibbetts, a high school freshman, asked the question, "How many of you parents would let your children hang around with dangerous people who might hurt them?" He paused, then added, "That's exactly what God did when he sent his son to earth."

But the religious authorities of Jesus' day did not see it that way. At the end of a desperate struggle on the part of the powers of this earth, Jesus was tried and executed on shaky legal grounds. Why would anyone want to kill a miracle worker, a healer, a teacher? Because the religious authorities of the day thought Jesus was the dangerous one, for he was critical of them.

Walter Wink, professor of biblical interpretation at Auburn Theological Seminary in New York, has suggested that for the powers of this earth it is an automatic reflex to suppress anyone who threatens the established order. Jesus posed a clear and present threat to the economic and political order. He proclaimed that the last would be first and the first last. He cast out the money changers from the Temple. Worst of all, he did not take the religious leaders seriously.

One thing is certain. The secret was out. With the crucifixion of Jesus, it was now possible to know the Messiah completely. But before the sacrifice on the cross that made the new covenant possible, Jesus celebrated the old covenant with his disciples. The Passover meal commemorates the hurried preparations God's people made in the middle of the night to escape Egypt and to shake off the bonds of slavery. Jesus took the symbols of passover and "baptized" them, making food and drink the memorials of his death and resurrection and the symbols of our escape from the slavery of sin to the freedom of grace.

The forms of our Passover, which we have come to call Communion, have changed over the years. Early Christians patterned this celebration after the feeding of the five thousand. As a matter of fact, early artistic renderings of the Lord's supper included the loaves and fishes as a matter of course. Male, female, slave, free, Jew, Gentile, rich, and poor, all were gathered together at one table to remember God through the bread and cup.

As time went by, this meal took on some of the characteristics of the pagan *refrigerarium*, or "refreshment" meal. This was a dinner shared with the dead, usually on the anniversary of their passing. Family and friends would gather to remember their departed loved ones, and in time the church community gathered periodically to remember those that the church body had lost to death.

Our communion meals are not usually as elaborate. However, when we eat a simple wafer with wine or grape juice or eat a full meal in remembrance of the sacrifice of Jesus, we are the body of Christ, sharing with the people around us, with Christians the world over, and with the most honored guest of all—the Word through whom all things were made, and without whom nothing was created.

After the command to do these things in remembrance of Jesus, Mark moved quickly on to the story of the crucifixion. His version of the execution is noteworthy because of the direct and understated way in which it was told. In contrast to the rest of the gospel, in which Jesus was the one who acted and shaped events, Jesus was the one acted upon here. He did nothing to resist as obscene tortures were forced upon him.

But one thing this gospel has in common with the other three accounts is that Jesus was abandoned by the twelve. This was part of the complete and utter failure of his worldly ministry. Those who had closest contact with him let him down. The inner circle could not stay awake during his time of trial, but it got worse. One betrayed him, one denied him, and the rest turned tail and ran. Only a few of the women remained, to look on from a distance.

And, consistent with the rest of the story, an outsider recognized Jesus for what he was. And not just any outsider. The centurion, one of those who participated in the execution, stated: "Truly this man was God's Son!" (15:39) The nations, even in their sin, have recognized that Jesus is Lord. This is the inner circle, the club into which we desire entry.

Is this a victory? Walter Wink addressed this question, noting first that the crucifixion of Jesus had changed everything. The crucifixion proved that death has no lasting effect. One might as well say that Martin Luther King Jr.'s life meant nothing because he had been killed, or that the lone, nameless student who for a few minutes held off the tanks in Tiananmen Square failed because the Chinese government killed thousands of students a few days later. In the end, the powers and principalities are powerless against those who do not fear death.

Luke's account of the early church, found in the Book of Acts, proved that persecution, far from eradicating the faith, only spread it farther. Eventually the Roman empire that crucified Jesus and the Temple authorities who conspired in the frame-up were no more. But we still recognize Jesus as Lord, which in no way romanticizes the obscenity of the cross.

My personal faith journey has taken me from one communion, the Roman Catholic Church, to another, the Church of the Brethren. Like every denomination, both are beloved of God and each has its own peculiar strengths and weaknesses. One of the few things I miss from my old church is that institution known as the "Stations of the Cross." Set at intervals in every Roman Catholic church are fourteen artistic representations of the torments of Jesus, leading up to and including the crucifixion.

It is all there: the crown of thorns, the flogging with the leather thongs—each tipped with a metal lug designed to flay, and the game soldiers played with a condemned prisoner, dressing him in colored robes and hailing him as king.

The prisoner carried his own crossbeam to the place of execution. There nails were plunged through his wrists into the beam, which was then pulled up by ropes on to the cross bar and nailed into place. The man's legs were drawn up until his knees were fairly bent, then a single nail was driven through the sides of both heels at once.

Eventually the condemned suffocated to death when he was too weak to pull himself up in agony in order to breathe. Little wonder that this horror was saved only for the dregs of society.

All of this makes the words of the Apostle Paul more powerful when he wrote, "I decided to know nothing among you except Jesus Christ, and him crucified." (1 Cor. 2:2)

How could anyone jump on that kind of bandwagon? Nowadays we who are separated from crucifixions by nearly 2,000 years think nothing of wearing the cross around our necks or on our lapels, and there is probably one on display in practically every church. But it was not always so. So shameful was the image of the cross, so obscene the method of execution, that it was not for over four centuries that the church chose to use that symbol in its art. The first example of the cross in art is in a piece of graffiti. It is a crude drawing. A man with the head of a donkey is being crucified. At his feet is an individual engaged in adoration. The legend, translated, reads: "Alexandros worships his god."

This anti-Christian drawing makes it clear how shameful the cross was. Yet this Alexandros was not ashamed to claim Jesus as Lord, even though it led to ridicule. And this is what Paul preached—admitting, even embracing, our shame, even as Christ paid the price so that we need feel our shame no more. Our faith is not for wimps.

The cross as an instrument of torture also represents the intersection of two roads. It is the place where heaven and earth come together. It is the spot where we meet Jesus. So Paul wrote that Jesus, "though he was in the form of God, did not regard equality with God as something to be exploited, but emptied himself, taking the form of a slave, being born in human likeness. And being found in human form, he humbled himself and became obedient to the point of death—even death on a cross." (Phil. 2:6-8) This is where we come together. At our broken points. This is where we have something in common.

How do we come to this intersection? One way is through our suffering. Much of our suffering is unsought, but it finds us anyway. There is no place in that dark valley where we will not find Jesus waiting.

Others among us arrive at this spot by taking upon ourselves the name of Jesus. To do so is to invite the world to crush us and ridicule us. Yet our lives are not spent in suffering. No one is called to intentionally seek out the experience of suffering. For those who are currently blessed with health in the midst of faithful living, there are other ways to join Jesus at the cross.

One way is through Communion. Whenever we break the bread and share the cup, we are proclaiming his death until he comes. Another way is through the service of anointing. Jesus was anointed by a woman who wished to serve him. Not only can we anoint each other for healing, but we can also serve each other as part of the cross we share.

The cross was supposed to eradicate the carpenter and all he stood for. It was supposed to end the problem, just as the deaths of Stephen, John, and the other martyrs were supposed to put an end to Christianity. Just tear it up by the roots and it will die, or so the Jewish authorities thought.

It does not work that way. I remember a scene a couple of years ago. I watched my neighbor down the road pull up dandelions to prevent their spread. Meanwhile, just a few yards away, my son Jacob was reciting what he had learned about dandelions at school the previous day—while blowing on the puffy heads to spread the seeds. Each seed caught the wind and was lost to sight as it sailed into the sun. No problem. There were going to be plenty more dandelions next spring.

That is the way it works. There is a stiff breeze blowing and it is impossible to put the seeds back on the stem. Jesus cannot be put back in the tomb.

Were you there when they crucified my Lord?

I hope so.

Discussion and Action

1. Read the paragraphs you wrote sharing your feelings about the crucifixion. Listen quietly as group members read. Do not question or comment until all are heard. Then reflect in silence on life.
2. Discuss how in your writing and your listening you have learned something new about this crucifixion account.
3. Identify the powers in this world that work against the faith. In what ways have they succeeded? Where do you see hope?
4. Where do you see Jesus suffering and dying in our world?
5. Who in your experience is living the cross? What can you do this week to help them walk the road to calvary?
6. Name ways you are called as Jesus' disciples to participate in his suffering and death.
7. Close again by singing "Were You There?"

10

He Is Not Here
Mark 16:1-20

The end of Mark does not reveal any ultimate truths.
The evangel has been revealing them all along. The end
launches us into the world, to trust the promise no
matter how hopeless or frightening it seems.

Personal Preparation

1. Read Mark 16:1-8. Your translation probably has a
   note at the bottom, telling you that this is where the
   gospel ends in the most ancient manuscripts. How does
   this ending make you feel? Where is the "good news"
   in it?
2. How does your translation handle the ending of Mark?
   If you have more than one translation at home, compare translations to see how Mark's gospel ends. In the
   longer ending (16:11-13), people had a hard time believing that Jesus was seen alive. Think of times it has
   been especially difficult for you to believe.
3. Was there a chapter in your life that ended abruptly?
   Prepare to share this in the group.

Understanding

Bob Dungy, former chaplain of the Upper Room, spoke to our
ministerial association about spiritual disciplines. He told a
story from his student days, when he grew impatient with God

for not speaking to him. A teacher suggested that he withdraw from his studies for an hour, review his shortcomings, and wait for God to speak.

Smiling, Dungy related how he reviewed his sins in just a few minutes, which left him most of an hour to stew and fret. As the hour drew to a close, he became angry that God did not speak directly, so he rose to complain to his teacher. All of a sudden, a message came from heaven.

Just two lines from a favorite hymn, "How Firm a Foundation": "What more can he say than to you he hath said, to you who for refuge to Jesus have fled?"

There was nothing more he could say, Dungy realized, when everything had been said to him over the course of his lifetime. And what more could Jesus say to us that he has not said through the first fifteen chapters of the Gospel of Mark?

The Gospel of Mark takes us to the edge of the resurrection and then breaks off abruptly. There are literally thousands of variants in the text of the entire Greek New Testament. Most of them are of little or no significance. But this variant in Mark is a big one. There was a time when the Revised Standard Version simply ended the gospel with verse 8, stowing verses 9-20 in a footnote. Later editions restored verses 9-20 to regular type. The New Revised Standard Version printed three different endings to the gospel, two in parentheses, and one in a footnote. Most other translations have done the same, with a few notable exceptions. William Lorimer's marvelous New Testament in Scots ends, "At that they came out o the graffchaumer an screived awa, trimmlin an 'maist by themsels wi feirich an dreid. An they tauld naebodie naething, sae afeard war they."

I have to say I am relieved about the traditional abrupt ending to Mark for one reason, that it removes that awful promise attributed to Jesus: "They will pick up snakes in their hands, and if they drink any deadly thing, it will not hurt them." (16:18)

The additional ending to the gospel as we have it is not particularly inspirational. There are familiar elements. Jesus appeared to Mary Magdalene and her report was received with skepticism. He met two disciples on the road but their report was not believed either. His appearance to the eleven included a version of the Great Commission and concluded with the ascension.

But there is nothing here we would not learn from the other gospels.

And more importantly, there is nothing here that Jesus did not already tell us during his lifetime. On three different occasions in the gospel, Jesus foretold his death and resurrection. At the transfiguration, the otherworldliness of Jesus was revealed.

Then on the day after the sabbath, the women arrived to find the stone rolled away and the tomb empty. What in heaven's name were they doing there? They did not know what would be waiting for them. As a matter of fact, they had no idea how they would get that stone moved. But they went. They were found at their post. Resurrection rewards those who are faithful, even when things seem hopeless.

A figure was waiting for them, "dressed in a white robe." (16:5) Just as bright as the clothes worn by Jesus, Moses, and Elijah in the transfiguration, his clothes proclaimed he was not of this earth. He said that Jesus was risen and that they would soon see him, "just as he told you." (16:7)

What more do you need than to you he has said? Because sooner or later your trust in the risen Lord has to begin. I am hesitant to quote from the gospel of John while working on a study of Mark, but the words of Jesus to Thomas are especially pertinent here: "Blessed are those who have not seen and yet have come to believe." (John 20:29)

It would be a rare Christian who did not wonder at some point what it would have been like to live during the time of Jesus. Despite what we may think, however, we cannot assume we would have been the ones who believed and understood. In Luke's parable of the rich man in hell, who begged for a sign to be given his survivors, Jesus had Abraham say, "If they do not listen to Moses and the prophets, neither will they be convinced even if someone rises from the dead." (Luke 16:31)

So the Gospel of Mark comes down to trust. You know where the story is heading. You get there. Do you believe? Faith calls for a leap in the dark. It is different than knowledge. I know in what part of the sky I can find the moon tonight. I know that my Redeemer lives. The same word, "know," is stated with the same certainty. One is based on scientific knowledge. The other is based on something else instead.

The crucial verse in the Gospel of Mark is the final one: "They said nothing to anyone, for they were afraid." (16:8) Of what were they afraid? Perhaps the new life.

Years ago, my wife Jennie was six months pregnant, in labor, and bleeding badly. After a tearful conversation with our doctor, we resigned ourselves to the fact our baby would not survive. Our attention was centered on how we could keep Jennie alive.

After further consideration the doctor came to us with an alternative. There was a slight possibility the infant might survive, in who knew what shape and at what cost, if Jennie were transported to a teaching hospital in a nearby city. No guarantees, not even much hope.

Suddenly the weight of the burden increased. The cost of life was going to be tremendous work. It involved the coincidental arrival of an ambulance, which broke every existing law to get us to the teaching hospital. It meant reopening every wound we thought we had temporarily closed. But it also meant life for Francisco, who at this writing is a fairly normal teenager, if the complaints of other parents are to be believed.

Most of us, even when our hearts are breaking, can handle disaster. We hunker down and absorb our losses. But there is something even more unsettling than catastrophe. It is what writer J.R.R. Tolkien called *eucatastrophe*—the good cataclysm. In his essay "On Fairy Stories" he wrote, "The Birth of Christ is the eucatastrophe of Man's history. The Resurrection is the eucatastrophe of the story of the Incarnation. This story begins and ends in joy."

The end of the gospel is not the end of the story, however. Resurrection is God's best shot. It is an attempt to get us in the ball game. Will it work? With the possibility of resurrection, we must be ready to make changes in our lives and lifestyles. Faced with the eucatastrophe of resurrection, we can no longer be satisfied with mediocrity.

He is risen! Will we have faith in a Christ we have not seen? Will we trust the Messiah's promise that death has been overcome, even at the moment that we feel most without hope? Will we live in the kingdom now, playing by kingdom rules?

What more can he say than to you he has said?

Discussion and Action

1. Read aloud together or listen as one person reads aloud Mark 16:1-8. Follow with a time of silence.
2. Read together "A Resurrection Liturgy," printed in the "General Sharing and Prayer Resources" section.
3. Discuss where the "good news" is in Mark's gospel, if verse 8 is the real end of his work?
4. Tell about a chapter in your life that ended abruptly. How did you respond? What did it take to recover and believe?
5. Resurrection means new life and more life. How will you work with your covenant group for new life and more life?
6. What did you learn from this study of Mark? What new things did you discover about Jesus? about yourself?
7. Close by singing "How Firm a Foundation." Pray for a complete understanding of Jesus.

Suggestions for Sharing and Prayer

This material is designed for covenant groups that spend one hour sharing and praying together, followed by one hour of Bible study. Some suggestions are offered here to help relate your sharing to your study of the Gospel of Mark. Session-by-session ideas are given first, followed by general resources. Use the ones you find most helpful. Also bring your own ideas for sharing and worshiping together in your covenant group.

1. The Beginning of the Good News

❑ Greet one another with one of the scripture sentences included in the general sharing and prayer resources.

❑ Form or renew your covenant together as a group. Use the suggestions from the general sharing and prayer ideas, or use your own covenant.

❑ Read aloud Psalm 119:105-112 in choral fashion, each member of the group reading a line and if possible sharing a sentence or thought about that line. Then reread it aloud together. God's word, which is the foundation of the covenant process, is a lamp for our feet and a light for our path.

❑ In groups of two or three, work at writing three-line biographies for each person in the group. Come together to share these.

❑ Close with one of the scriptural prayers and a benediction, printed in the general resources section.

2. The Time Is Up!

❑ Greet one another with one of the scriptural sentences from the general resources or use one you found yourself.

❑ Sing "Amazing Grace" together. Many will know the first verse by heart. If possible sing without a hymnal.

❑ On newsprint, make a list of every conceivable title for members in the group, such as Mrs., Dr., Dad, plumber, first baseman, or Mary. How do these define who we are? Do they limit us? This lesson's passage from Mark lists a couple of the titles for Jesus. What do they say about him?

❑ "Roughing it" is sometimes used as an image for the incarnation. The Greek word for "dwelt" (as in "The word was made flesh and dwelt among us") suggests pitching a tent and recalls the Exodus of God's people, when the tabernacle had to be as movable as the rest of the camp. Tell about camping experiences and how roughing it changes one's perspective.

❑ Read aloud Psalm 25:1-10. Allow each person to read a line and comment on it; then read it in unison. God does not forget his people. Jesus comes just in time.

❑ Close with a scripture prayer and a benediction.

3. We've Never Seen Anything Like This

❑ Greet one another with a scriptural sentence.

❑ In groups of two or three, share prayer requests. These can also be used in the anointing service that follows.

❑ Come together to share in an anointing service. See the general resources section for a sample service. Both spoken and unspoken prayer requests can be the subject for prayer in this service.

❑ Read Psalm 147:1-11 in the manner of the previous psalms. God gathers the outcasts. God is good to us.

❑ Explore actions that members of the group have taken in the name of the gospel that have offended others. Are

there actions you would like to have taken but did not?
What are they?

❑ What project needs to be done for the church that your
group could perform, some ministry the church is
lacking? Consider doing it.

❑ Close with a scripture prayer and a benediction.

4. Who Then Is This?

❑ Greet one another with a scriptural sentence. Test your
memory. See if you can use the scriptural greetings
without reading them from the book.

❑ Bring chess pieces or children's play figures. Use them to
act out a portion of this session's scriptures from Mark.
Have someone read the passage from the Bible as
someone else is moving the figures.

❑ Write your own parable as a group. Focus on a sin of
which you and your church are guilty.

❑ This week's psalm is 50:1-6, "Our God comes and does
not keep silence." (Ps. 50:3) Read the psalm aloud and
say in sentence prayers what God is telling us in these
days.

❑ Close with a scripture prayer. For your benediction, use
"And I Will Raise You Up," "Lo, a Gleam from Yonder
Heaven," or "He Leadeth Me." Pray the words together
or learn the song and sing it as your prayer.

5. Do You Not Yet Understand?

❑ Open with scriptural sentences. Try to recite them
without referring to the book. See if you can recite
different ones.

❑ Today's psalm is very brief. Psalm 117 is only two verses
long and looks toward the time God is praised by all
peoples, not simply a single nation. You might

experiment with this psalm, each person reading it individually in an effort to emphasize different words. Reread it until you can all speak it from memory. Or try chanting it, or singing it to a folk tune such as "Three Blind Mice."

❑ Make a list called "Tender Mercies" on a sheet of newsprint. List the times you believe God has intervened in your life, answered prayer, or blessed your life.

❑ Read Hebrews 13:2. Make a second list called "Entertaining Angels." List those times you have been of service to others. Were they aware of it at the time? Tell stories about odd or angelic encounters.

❑ You may wish to include a fellowship meal as part of this hour. God is worshiped in the meals we share together.

❑ Use the chess pieces or children's storytelling figures to recreate the two feeding stories.

❑ Close with a scripture prayer and a song or benediction such as "Go Now in Peace" or "God Be with You 'til We Meet Again."

6. You Are the Messiah!

❑ Greet each other with scriptural sentences. Vary them, taking a phrase from one and a phrase from the other. Try singing them or chanting them.

❑ Psalm 131 is the focus of sharing this week. Before you read the psalm together, talk about your schedules for the week. Then have three people read one verse each of Psalm 131. Pause between verses for silent prayer.

❑ Have each person in the circle ask, "Who do you say that I am?" Let everyone share some reflection or observation about that individual.

❑ Hold a feetwashing service in imitation of Jesus. A feetwashing service is included in the general resources section.

❑ Close with a scriptural prayer and "Guide My Feet."

7. By What Authority Are You Doing these Things?

❑ Greet each other with scriptural sentences.

❑ Examine each other's key rings. Over what do they give you authority? How do you use that authority?

❑ If your group had a million dollars to sponsor a ministry for the church, name ways you would spend it. What do these ideas say about your group? What could you do with a smaller amount? Consider doing it.

❑ Recite Psalm 61. The psalmist found refuge in God and asked God for protection for the king as well. For whom do you wish protection and guidance? In prayer, take turns saying how God is a refuge for you.

❑ If you were to choose a name for your covenant group, what name would describe who you are or who you want to be? Make suggestions and then use paper and markers to design a logo for the group.

❑ Sing "Amazing Grace" and close with a scriptural prayer.

8. Do Not Be Alarmed

❑ Greet each other in your own words, imitating the scriptural sentences. Write down the ones you like best and keep them for other occasions.

❑ Listen to and meditate on a recording of "Worthy Is the Lamb," from Handel's *Messiah*.

❑ Psalm 121 contains the assurance that God is with us on the journey to the Temple. After reciting the psalm, read

aloud Revelation 20—21. Now describe the journey to
the new Temple in your own words.

❑ In pairs or groups of three, name the things you
personally would like to find in the New Jerusalem. Talk
about what constitutes heaven for you. How do the group
members' images compare? Come back together and tell
of the images of heaven you like best.

❑ Pray for God's kingdom and for each person in the group
as they live toward the New Jerusalem.

❑ Close with a scriptural prayer and a benediction.

9. Truly This Was God's Son

❑ Gather in silence. Pray silently for each other. Reflect on
those burdens that other members of your group bear.
Are there members of the group about whom you know
very little? Pray also for them.

❑ Recite Psalm 22:1-2 several times as a group. Begin softly
and build in volume until you are practically shouting.
Then lower the volume until there is silence. Recite it
silently until an appointed leader brings the psalm to a
halt.

❑ If you have access to a booklet on the Stations of the
Cross, share with the group the event at each station. If
not, use the scriptures for this session and name the
sufferings of Jesus. Pause between each to allow
members of the group to meditate aloud on each of
Jesus' sacrifices.

❑ Close with "O Sacred Head, Now Wounded" or "Were
You There?" leaving out the final verse about
resurrection.

10. He Is Not Here

❑ Greet one another as if the close of the age is at hand.

❑ Read singly and as a group Psalm 118:17-24. The psalmist said, "I shall not die but I shall live." (Ps. 118:17) Share with each other the certainty you have that you "shall live."

❑ Sing "Were You There?" including the resurrection verse, singing it with energy and fire. Then sing with force "I Know That My Redeemer Lives."

❑ Close with a scriptural prayer and a benediction. Since this is the last meeting on Mark, you may want to speak your own prayers of blessing or benediction for each person, while lightly laying hands on each one's head or shoulders.

General Sharing and Prayer Resources

Forming a Covenant Group
Covenant Expectations
Covenant-making is significant throughout the biblical story. God made covenants with Noah, Abraham, and Moses. Jeremiah spoke about God making a covenant with the people, "written on the heart." In the New Testament, Jesus was identified as the mediator of the New Covenant, and the early believers lived out of covenant relationships. Throughout history people have lived in covenant relationship with God and within community.

Christians today also covenant with God and make commitments to each other. Such covenants help believers live out their faith. God's empowerment comes to them as they gather in covenant communities to pray and study, share and receive, reflect and act.

People of the Covenant is a program that is anchored in this covenantal history of God's people. It is a network of covenantal relationships. Denominations, districts or regions, congregations, small groups, and individuals all make covenants. Covenant group members commit themselves to the mission statement, seeking to become more:

- biblically informed so they better understand the revelation of God;

- globally aware so they know themselves to be better connected with all of God's world;

- relationally sensitive to God, self, and others.

The Burlap Cross Symbol
The imperfections of the burlap cross, its rough texture and unrefined fabric, the interweaving of threads, the uniqueness of each strand, are elements that are present within the covenant group. The people in the groups are imperfect, unpolished, interrelated with each other, yet still unique beings.

The shape that this collection of imperfect threads creates is the cross, symbolizing for all Christians the resurrection and presence of Christ our Savior. A covenant group is something akin to this burlap cross. It unites common, ordinary people and sends them out again in all directions to be in the world.

A Litany of Commitment

All: We are a people of the covenant; out of our commitment to Christ, we seek to become:

Group 1:   more biblically informed so we understand better God's revelation;

Group 2:   more globally aware so we know ourselves connected with all of God's people;

Group 1:   more relationally sensitive to God, self, and others.

All: We are a people of the covenant; we promise:

Group 2:   to seek ways of living out and sharing our faith;

Group 1:   to participate actively in congregational life;

Group 2:   to be open to the leading of the Spirit in our lives.

All: We are a people of the covenant; we commit our-
            selves:

Group 1:   to attend each group meeting, so far as possible;

Group 2:   to prepare through Bible study, prayer, and action;

Group 1:   to share thoughts and feelings, as appropriate;

Group 2:   to encourage each other on our faith journeys.

All: We are a people of the covenant.

> The preceding information and Litany of Commitment are from
> the People of the Covenant program, Church of the Brethren
> General Board, 1451 Dundee Avenue, Elgin, Illinois 60120.

A Covenant Prayer

O God, we renew the covenant
spoken by our fathers and mothers,
   sung in homes and meeting houses,
   written by the pens of pilgrims and preachers.
This covenant we know is costly;
   but there is another of greater value.
So we accept your gifts and promises
   with thanksgiving;
and offer you our lives and our love. Amen.

> By Leland Wilson. Adapted from *The Gifts We Bring,* Volume 2
> (Worship Resources for Stewardship and Mission).

Through the Week

Develop a list of scriptural greetings, prayers, and benedictions
from the Bible to add to the ones provided here. To get started,
look at the openings and closings of Paul's letters.

An Invocation
■ Let the words of my mouth and the meditation of my heart
be acceptable to you, O Lord, my rock and my redeemer.
(Ps. 19:14)

Sentences for Greeting
■ Grace to you and peace from God our Father and the Lord
Jesus Christ. (1 Cor. 1:3)

■ Grace, mercy, and peace will be with us from God the Father and from Jesus Christ, the Father's Son, in truth and love. (2 John 1:3)

■ Grace to you and peace from him who is and who was and who is to come, and from the seven spirits who are before his throne. (Rev. 1:4)

Scripture Prayers
■ Our Father which art in heaven,
Hallowed be thy name.
Thy kingdom come.
Thy will be done in earth, as it is in heaven.
Give us this day our daily bread.
And forgive us our debts, as we forgive our debtors.
And lead us not into temptation, but deliver us from evil:
For thine is the kingdom, and the power, and the glory, for ever. Amen. (Matt. 6:9-13 KJV)

■ Father, hallowed be your name. Your kingdom come.
Give us each day our daily bread.
And forgive us our sins, for we ourselves forgive everyone indebted to us. And do not bring us to the time of trial. (Luke 11:2-4)

Benedictions
■ The Lord bless you and keep you; the Lord make his face to shine upon you, and be gracious to you; the Lord lift up his countenance upon you, and give you peace. (Num. 6:24-26)

■ Now to God who is able to strengthen you according to my gospel and the proclamation of Jesus Christ, according to the revelation of the mystery that was kept secret for long ages but is now disclosed, and through the prophetic writings is made known to all the Gentiles, according to the command of the eternal God, to bring about the obedience of faith—to the only wise God, through Jesus Christ, to whom be the glory forever! Amen. (Rom. 16:25-27)

■ Now to him who is able to keep you from falling, and to make you stand without blemish in the presence of his glory with rejoicing, to the only God our Savior, through Jesus Christ our Lord, be glory, majesty, power, and authority, before all time and now and forever. Amen. (Jude 24-25)

Psalms for This Series

■ Your word is a lamp to my feet and a light to my path.
I have sworn an oath and confirmed it, to observe your
    righteous ordinances.
I am severely afflicted; give me life, O Lord, according to
    your word.
Accept my offerings of praise, O Lord, and teach me your
    ordinances.
I hold my life in my hand continually, but I do not forget your
    law.
The wicked have laid a snare for me, but I do not stray from
    your precepts.
Your decrees are my heritage forever; they are the joy of my
    heart.
I incline my heart to perform your statutes forever, to the
    end. (Ps. 119:105-112)

■ To you, O Lord, I lift up my soul.
O my God, in you I trust; do not let me be put to shame; do
    not let my enemies exult over me.
Do not let those who wait for you be put to shame; let them
    be ashamed who are wantonly treacherous.
Make me to know your ways, O Lord; teach me your paths.
Lead me in your truth, and teach me, for you are the God of
    my salvation; for you I wait all day long.
Be mindful of your mercy, O Lord, and of your steadfast love,
    for they have been from of old.
Do not remember the sins of my youth or my transgressions;
    according to your steadfast love remember me, for your
    goodness' sake, O Lord!
Good and upright is the Lord; therefore he instructs sinners
    in the way.
He leads the humble in what is right, and teaches the humble
    his way.
All the paths of the Lord are steadfast love and faithfulness,
    for those who keep his covenant and his decrees. (Ps. 25:1-10)

■ Praise the Lord! How good it is to sing praises to our God;
    for he is gracious, and a song of praise is fitting.
The Lord builds up Jerusalem; he gathers the outcasts of
    Israel.
He heals the brokenhearted, and binds up their wounds.

He determines the number of the stars; he gives to all of
  them their names.
Great is our Lord, and abundant in power; his understanding
  is beyond measure.
The Lord lifts up the downtrodden; he casts the wicked to
  the ground.
Sing to the Lord with thanksgiving; make melody to our God
  on the lyre.
He covers the heavens with clouds, prepares rain for the
  earth, makes grass grow on the hills.
He gives to the animals their food, and to the young ravens
  when they cry.
His delight is not in the strength of the horse, nor his
  pleasure in the speed of a runner;
but the Lord takes pleasure in those who fear him, in those
  who hope in his steadfast love. (Ps. 147:1-11)

■ The mighty one, God the Lord, speaks and summons the
  earth from the rising of the sun to its setting.
Out of Zion, the perfection of beauty, God shines forth.
Our God comes and does not keep silence, before him is a
  devouring fire, and a mighty tempest all around him.
He calls to the heavens above and to the earth, that he may
  judge his people:
"Gather to me my faithful ones, who made a covenant with
  me by sacrifice!"
The heavens declare his righteousness, for God himself is
  judge. *Selah*. (Ps. 50:1-6)

■ Praise the Lord, all you nations! Extol him, all you peoples!
For great is his steadfast love toward us, and the faithfulness
  of the Lord endures forever. Praise the Lord! (Ps. 117)

■ O Lord, my heart is not lifted up, my eyes are not raised too
  high; I do not occupy myself with things too great and too
  marvelous for me.
But I have calmed and quieted my soul, like a weaned child
  with its mother; my soul is like the weaned child that is with
  me.
O Israel, hope in the Lord from this time on and
forevermore. (Ps. 131)

■ Hear my cry, O God; listen to my prayer.
From the end of the earth I call to you, when my heart is
  faint. Lead me to the rock that is higher than I;
for you are my refuge, a strong tower against the enemy.
Let me abide in your tent forever, find refuge under the
  shelter of your wings. *Selah.*
For you, O God, have heard my vows; you have given me the
  heritage of those who fear your name.
Prolong the life of the king; may his years endure to all
  generations!
May he be enthroned forever before God; appoint steadfast
  love and faithfulness to watch over him!
So I will always sing praises to your name, as I pay my vows
  day after day. (Ps. 61)

■ I lift up my eyes to the hills—from where will my help come?
My help comes from the Lord, who made heaven and earth.
He will not let your foot be moved; he who keeps you will not
  slumber.
He who keeps Israel will neither slumber nor sleep.
The Lord is your keeper; the Lord is your shade at your right
  hand.
The sun shall not strike you by day, nor the moon by night.
The Lord will keep you from all evil; he will keep your life.
The Lord will keep your going out and your coming in from
  this time on and forevermore. (Ps. 121)

■ My God, my God, why have you forsaken me? Why are you
  so far from helping me, from the words of my groaning?
O my God, I cry by day, but you do not answer; and by night,
  but find no rest. (Ps. 22:1-2)

■ I shall not die, but I shall live, and recount the deeds of the
  Lord.
The Lord has punished me severely, but he did not give me
  over to death.
Open to me the gates of righteousness, that I may enter
  through them and give thanks to the Lord.
This is the gate of the Lord; the righteous shall enter
  through it.
I thank you that you have answered me and have become my
  salvation.

The stone that the builders rejected has become the chief
   cornerstone.
This is the Lord's doing; it is marvelous in our eyes.
This is the day that the Lord has made; let us rejoice and be
   glad in it. (Ps. 118:17-24)

Liturgy for Anointing
Read aloud Lamentations 3:19-24 or James 5:13-16.

Leader: We are gathered together to anoint our (brother/sis-
          ter) in the presence of God. We come boldly forward
          with courage because Jesus commanded us to pray,
          "Give us this day our daily bread." We come meekly
          with the fears of Jesus when he prayed, "Not my will,
          but thine." Knowing that in the midst of a broken
          world God wills your wholeness in body, mind, and
          spirit, I now anoint you with oil [the leader anoints
          the forehead in the shape of three crosses] for the
          forgiveness of your sins, the granting of peace to your
          soul, and the restoration of wholeness to your body.

[The leader then lays hands on the head of the one being
anointed. Others present may also lay their hands upon the
anointed or upon the shoulder of a neighbor until all are
connected by touch. After the leader's prayer, a silence follows
in which others may pray aloud or silently as they choose. The
leader closes with a brief spoken prayer, followed by the Lord's
Prayer in which all may join.]

A Feetwashing Service
Gather together in a circle. Have one member read John 13:1-
17 aloud. Wrapping an apronlike towel around the waist, and
taking a towel in hand, the first person washes the feet of the
person next to him or her, using a basin of water and drying the
feet with the towel. After the feet are washed, the washer and
the washed stand and embrace. If they wish, they may share the
Holy Kiss. Then the person whose feet have just been washed
takes the towel and turns to wash the feet of the next person,
and so on around the circle. During the rite, sing or hum hymns
the group knows from memory.

A Resurrection Liturgy

Leader: When the women found the empty tomb, they were
            led to this conclusion:

All: He is risen!

Leader: When Mary Magdalene found him in the garden, she
            knew it was true that:

All: He is risen!

Leader: When Peter's tongue was loosed by the descent of
            the Spirit, and he preached to each in his own lan-
            guage, his message was this:

All: He is risen!

Leader: Before pen was put to paper, before there was a gos-
            pel, or a letter, or a revelation to John, there was this
            message of Christianity:

All: He is risen!

Leader: Though our ancestors in the faith were hunted and
            killed, they embraced their deaths gladly with this
            promise on their lips:

All: He is risen!

Leader: Before there were Catholics and Protestants, before
            there were Baptists and Disciples and Brethren,
            bishops and popes and general ministers and general
            secretaries and presidents, before there were clergy
            and laity, there was this proclamation:

All: He is risen!

Leader: It happened in one place and in one time, for all
            times. It will not listen to hopelessness. It is the core,
            the message of salvation; it was planned from the be-
            ginning by God, and fulfilled in the end for us. Shout
            it from the mountaintops so that all may hear that:

All: He is risen! Christ the Lord is risen today! He is
            risen! Amen!

Liturgy for the Fellowship Meal

If the group chooses to share a fellowship meal as suggested for lesson 5, the group may wish to use this liturgy. This responsive reading is taken from the *Didake*, a church manual with materials dating back perhaps to 60 A.D. Here is the text for the cup and bread:

Leader: And regarding the thanksgiving (Eucharist), give thanks in this way.
          Regarding first the cup—we give thanks to you, our Father, for the holy vine of your servant David, which you revealed fully in Jesus your servant.

All: Glory to you forever.

Leader: And regarding the broken bread—we give thanks to you, our Father, for the life and the knowledge you have made known to us through your servant Jesus.

All: Glory to you forever.

Leader: For as this bread was once scattered over the mountains but was brought together into one loaf, so too gather your fellowship from the four corners of the world into your kingdom.

All: For yours are the glory and the power through Jesus Christ, forever.

[The meal follows. The *Didake* gives these instructions for after the meal. This is how you should give thanks after everyone is full.]

Leader: Holy Father, we give thanks to you for your holy name, which you have planted in our hearts, and for the knowledge and faith and eternal life you have made known through Jesus your servant.

All: Glory to you forever.

Leader: All-powerful ruler, who made everything with your name in mind, you gave people food and drink to make us glad so they could thank you for it. And to us you have given spiritual food and drink and eternal life, through your servant Jesus. We thank you most of all for being all powerful.

All: Glory to you forever.

Leader: Remember your church, Lord, and preserve it from evil, perfecting it in your love, and gathering it from the four winds, in holiness, into your kingdom which you have prepared for it.

All: For yours is the power and the glory, forever.

Leader: Let your grace come, let this world pass away.

All: Hosanna to the Son of David.

Leader: If anyone is holy, let them approach. If anyone is not, let them repent. *Maranatha*—come soon, Lord. Amen.

(Translated from the Greek by Frank Ramirez.)

I Know That My Redeemer Lives
SHOUT ON, PRAY ON LM with refrains

1 I know that my Re - deem-er lives,
2 He lives to bless me with his love, glo - ry, hal - le - lu - jah!
3 He lives, all glo-ry to his name, lu - jah!

What com - fort this sweet sen-tence gives,
He lives to plead for me a - bove, glo - ry, hal - le - lu - jah!
He lives, my Sav - ior, still the same, lu - jah!

Shout on, pray on, we're gain - ing ground,
He lives, my hun - gry soul to feed, glo - ry, hal - le - lu - jah!
What joy the bless'd as - sur - ance gives,
O pray on, we're gain - ing ground,
yes he lives, my soul to feed,
joy the blest as - sur - ance gives,

The dead's a - live and the lost is found,
He lives, to help in time of need, glo - ry, hal - le - lu - jah!
I know that my Re - deem-er lives, lu - jah!
dead's a - live the lost is found,
lives to help in time of need,
know that my Re - deem-er lives,

Text: Samuel Medley, *Psalms and Hymns*, 1775, alt.

Music: *Sacred Harp*, 2nd ed., 1850
Harmonization copyright © 1988 Alice Parker. Used with permission.

Were You There
WERE YOU THERE Irregular

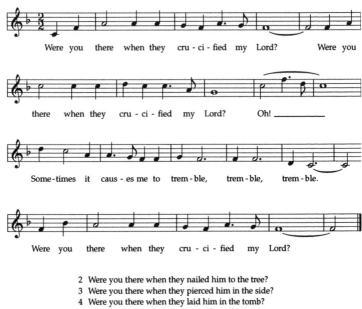

Were you there when they cru - ci - fied my Lord? Were you
there when they cru - ci - fied my Lord? Oh! _____
Some-times it caus - es me to trem - ble, trem - ble, trem - ble.
Were you there when they cru - ci - fied my Lord?

2 Were you there when they nailed him to the tree?
3 Were you there when they pierced him in the side?
4 Were you there when they laid him in the tomb?
5 Were you there when he rose up from the dead?

Text: African-American spiritual, *Old Plantation Hymns*, 1899
Music: African-American spiritual, *Folk Songs of the American Negro*, 1907

Amazing Grace
NEW BRITAIN (AMAZING GRACE) CM

Text: John Newton (Sts. 1-5), *Olney Hymns*, 1779; A Collection of Sacred Ballads (St. 6), 1790

Music: American folk melody, *Virginia Harmony*, 1831; adapted and harmonized by Edwin O. Excell, 1900

Guide My Feet
GUIDE MY FEET Irregular

2 Hold my hand...
3 Stand by me...
4 I'm your child...
5 Search my heart...

Text: African-American spiritual

Music: African-American spiritual
         Harmonization copyright © Wendell Whalum